Finding Joy When Life is Out of Focus

Finding Joy When Life is Out of Focus

Angela Donadio

BRIDGE LOGOS

Newberry, FL 32669

Bridge-Logos
Newberry, FL 32669

Finding Joy When Life is Out of Focus:
Philippians—A Study for Joy-Thirsty Women
by Angela Donadio

Printed in the United States of America

Library of Congress Catalog Card Number: 2018931860

International Standard Book Number: 978-1-61036-993-0

Cover and interior design by: Kent Jensen | knail.com

Dedication

To Dale, my husband and partner for life. Thank you for believing in me and supporting me through thick and thin. "Attraversiamo…I love you."

To Gabrielle and Christian, who continually inspire me to dream for more and challenge me to never settle. You're amazing and I love being your mom.

Acknowledgements

Thank you, Jesus. You relentlessly pursue this joy-thirsty girl. You know me better than anyone else and love me best. Use my words to deposit Your story in the heart of every joy-thirsty woman.

Thank you, Dale. Your love steadies me through every adventure. I love doing life with you. None of this would be the same without you.

Thank you, Gabrielle and Christian. You've taken this journey with me and I'm forever grateful. No matter what happens in life, keep your compass pointed north to Jesus.

Thank you, Mom and Dad. You invested your time, energy, love, resources, and most of all—Jesus—into my life. Watching you weather life's challenges framed the way I view my own. "Through it all, I've learned to trust in Jesus, I've learned to trust in God." Thank you to extended family and family in heaven. Who even knows where I would be without your prayers.

Thank you, River of Life Family. You've had a front row seat to every dark valley and steep mountain climb. You've carried me through seasons of unbelievable difficulty and unbridled joy with open arms. I'm truly blessed.

Thank you, my River of Life "Finding Joy" girls! Thank you to those who bravely tackled my first draft, led the original studies, and served on my launch team! Your insights and suggestions fill these pages. Thank you, Janet, for being the best friend a girl could ask for. Thank you, Miriam, for your painstaking assistance on this manuscript and for guarding my sanity. Thank you, Izla, for your patience and editing expertise. You're the reason my editor had so little to do.

Thank you to those who graciously extended your endorsement of this book. I admire your leadership and unwavering faith more than you'll ever know.

Thank you, Jim Hart at Hartline Agency. Your guidance as my agent has been invaluable. You've helped me to stay true to my convictions and pursue my calling.

Thank you, Suzi Wooldridge and the Bridge Logos Family. I'm over the moon to take this journey with you and look forward to future endeavors together!

Endorsements

Is it possible to have true joy in the midst of tough times? I've personally wrestled with this question and Angela has too. It's from that place of struggle turned strength that Angela beautifully points us to our ultimate Source of lasting joy no matter what circumstance we might face.

—**LYSA TERKEURST,** NEW YORK TIMES BESTSELLING AUTHOR AND PRESIDENT OF PROVERBS 31 MINISTRIES

I loved serving at Angela's church! She is so full of love and life and... surprises! When our worship leader's accompanist's flight was delayed, Angela stepped right up and played the keyboard as if she'd rehearsed her whole life just for that one night! It was just one more indication that she is gifted by God and ready to serve however and whenever He calls! I am blessed to call her my sister in Christ.

—**JENNIFER ROTHSCHILD,** AUTHOR OF ME, MYSELF & LIES: WHAT TO SAY WHEN YOU TALK TO YOURSELF, AND LESSONS I LEARNED IN THE DARK: STEPS TO WALKING BY FAITH NOT BY SIGHT, WWW.JENNIFERROTHSCHILD.COM

When we pray, the Lord may change our circumstances or change us in the circumstances. Angela Donadio's powerful and insightful walk through Paul's letter to the Philippians focuses on the latter. The Apostle wrote from prison where his circumstances weren't changing—yet his letter to the Philippians shares the joy of who he is, who he is with and the place he's in. *Finding Joy When Life is Out of Focus* will help you to do the same as the Apostle. I highly recommend this book.

—**DR. GEORGE O. WOOD,** FORMER CHAIRMAN, WORLD ASSEMBLIES OF GOD FELLOWSHIP, AUTHOR OF *ROAD TRIP LEADERSHIP, LIVING IN THE SPIRIT, A PSALM IN YOUR HEART, LIVING FULLY, THE SUCCESSFUL LIFE,* AND A COLLEGE TEXT ON THE BOOK OF ACTS

I absolutely LOVED this Bible study. Angela has a powerful way of unpacking the Word and thoughtfully asking the hard questions that ultimately help bring our lives back into focus. She constantly challenged me to go deeper into the understanding and truths of Philippians and how I, too, can find fullness of joy in the midst of my own disappointments, hurts, failures and struggles AND keep it. This was a life-transforming study for me and I am certain it will do the same for you as your lens and perspectives change.

—**TAMMY TRENT,** SINGER, SONGWRITER, AUTHOR OF *LEARNING TO BREATHE AGAIN,* AND *BEYOND THE SORROW: THERE'S HOPE IN THE PROMISES OF GOD*

Angela Donadio shows us that joy isn't a treasure lying on the surface to be lightly picked up and pocketed. Instead, she takes us deep into the truths of Philippians, mining sparkling nuggets of joy as we go.

—**AMY CARROLL,** AUTHOR OF BREAKING UP WITH PERFECT, PROVERBS 31 MINISTRIES SPEAKER AND WRITER

Angela is the real deal—she has experienced thirst and found fountains to drink from. Her book is her way of sharing this abundant supply of refreshment with all who come thirsting for joy. I invite you to take a drink. You will be refreshed, transformed and challenged to see life from God's perspective.

Most people want to love the life they live, but struggle to see theirs through God's lens. When walking through disappointment, worry and adversity, it is easy to see through a blurry lens that distorts our perspective. *Finding Joy When Life is Out of Focus* by Angela Donadio dives into the book of Philippians finding treasures of truth that will speak life and hope to your soul while providing tools and thought-provoking questions to dig for the gold in God's Word.

—**RUTH PULEO,** PRESENTLY WOMEN OF PURPOSE DIRECTOR FOR THE PENNDEL MINISTRIES NETWORK OF THE ASSEMBLIES OF GOD, ORDAINED MINISTER, SPEAKER, WRITER, WORLD MISSIONS FOCUS, FORMERLY ASSOCIATE PASTOR WITH HER HUSBAND OF 40 YEARS, MOTHER OF THREE, AND GRANDMOTHER OF EIGHT

The unsearchable riches of Christ's life and love are discovered by people such as Angela as a result of trials and testings. It is out of these experiences that Angela writes for joy-thirsty women. As you read this book, take time for the Holy Spirit to compact the truths into your heart, soul, and mind; and as a result you, too, will have the life changing power of the Word of God, the real life victories that have resulted in the life and ministry of Angela. Because of the thirst that the Spirit birthed in the author's heart, she now writes not just words to fill a book; but she sincerely desires for those who are hungry to live a life in Jesus to its fullest. This joy is given to those who are thirsty, for Jesus said in John 15:11: "These things have I spoken unto you that my joy might remain in you, and that your joy might be full."

—**DR. THOMAS TRASK,** FORMER CHAIRMAN, WORLD ASSEMBLIES OF GOD FELLOWSHIP. AUTHOR OF *FRUIT OF THE SPIRIT: BECOMING THE PERSON GOD WANTS YOU TO BE, THE BATTLE: DEFEATING THE ENEMIES OF YOUR SOUL, BACK TO THE ALTAR, THE CHOICE,* AND *THE BLESSING.*

This is a page-turning well written workbook with a narrative that will reach women from all walks of life. For each week, there is a true-to-life lesson that helps me find joy in seasons when my career path puts a demand on my focus and the highest expression of talents. Pastor Angela equips you with succinctly compiled material to help you begin a journey that creates opportunities for practical application of scripture. The context of the living, powerful and energetic word of God has been structured to be received with an attitude of meekness, reverence and the fear of God. Even as the entrance of God's word continuously gives light and understanding, the reader sees themselves as part of a single comprehensive joy filled plan of God that spans the universe. Finding their place in this joyful divine plan, readers achieve a sense of self-worth and personal fulfillment that satisfies their deepest longings for continuous joy.

Scripture compares the word of God to a mirror that reveals our outer appearance for adjustment. As I read this book, I encountered the mirror for my soul; the book of Philippians revealed my inward spiritual nature and condition. In the same way that I attend to anything my external mirror reveals without delay, I continue to attend to areas that need nourishment and adjustment so that I maintain continuous joy especially when my focus is challenged.

—**ESTHER GATUMA,** BRITISH COMPUTING SOCIETY FELLOW (FBCS), PMP, CSM, SAFE
OPRAH WINFREY SHOW SEASON 25 HERO

Let's be honest. In the real world (yeah...*this* one) we all go through times when, due to circumstances beyond our control, joy is harder to find than a lost contact lens on an ice skating rink. And with that loss of joy, there goes our perspective—our ability to focus on the things that really matter, that will sustain us through adversity.

In *Finding Joy When Life Is Out of Focus: Philippians—A Study for Joy-Thirsty Women* by my friend Angela Donadio, we find hope that trouble can be paired with triumph, loss with learning, pain with praise. Throughout the pages of *Finding Joy*, Angela skillfully weaves the biblical truths that sustained and transformed her with her own personal story of agonizing struggle through two life-threatening illnesses. But this is anything but a *'poor me'* book. This practical yet profound study of Philippians will help spiritually-thirsty women everywhere find their way forward into new seasons of regained focus and rediscovered joy, just as Angela did. Yes, even in the real world.

—**DR. JODI DETRICK,** AUTHOR OF *THE JESUS-HEARTED WOMAN*, SPEAKER, FORMER
SEATTLE TIMES COLUMNIST, WWW.JODIDETRICK.COM

It has been a joy to know Angela and her husband, Pastor Dale Donadio. I have seen her go through some very challenging and life-threatening illnesses, and yet she has come out of them with greater strength, joy and vitality. Angela is a brilliant writer, and effective communicator. This is an inspiring book-we all need to find a little more joy as we face life filled with many challenges, disappointments and adversities. Be blessed!'

—**ELIO MARROCCO,** LEAD MINISTER NEW LIFE CHRISTIAN CHURCH BA, DIPED,
DIPTHEOL, DIPCOUNS

Contents

Introduction

STUDY PROMPTS

USING THE "3 A'S" TO ENRICH YOUR STUDY

We will study the Book of Philippians verse-by-verse, focusing on key points as we go. One of the advantages of going through Scripture slowly is the ability to understand each passage to its fullest. This study uses the NIV Study Bible, 2002 Edition.

We will use "3 A's" as Study Prompts as we cover the following chapters together:

- Sessions 1-3, Chapter 1
- Sessions 4-5, Chapter 2
- Sessions 6-7, Chapter 3
- Sessions 8-9, Chapter 4

The "3 A's" will guide you to get the most out of your study. Before you begin to read any passage of Scripture, analyze the verse or passage. Context is critical to discovering the author of the book, the period of time and location surrounding its writing, and the reasons the author wrote it.

STUDY PROMPTS: THE 3 A'S

AMPLIFY

Amplify the text: Identify and focus on key words and phrases in the verses you are studying. What stands out to you? What are the main concepts?

APPLY

Apply what you've learned: Information only becomes transformation when you seek application. Identify how the text is relevant to your own life.

ASK

Ask questions: Dig deeper into God's Word by asking questions, both of God and of yourself. What changes do you need to make to take hold of the wisdom, power, and promises you uncovered in the passage?

Joy-thirsty women, **"Finding Joy"** will inspire you to look through the lens of God's perspective and love the life you see!

— *Session 1* —

Shackled and Singing

FINDING JOY IN ADVERSITY
PHILIPPIANS CHAPTER 1

DAY 1 / AN UNFORGETTABLE FIRST IMPRESSION—CH 1:1-2

DAY 2 / BEHIND THE TAPESTRIED DRAPES

DAY 3 / PRIORITY OF PRAYER

DAY 4 / GOD'S WAITING ROOM—CH 1:6-8

DAY 5 / LOVE THAT OVERFLOWS—CH 1:9-11

An Unforgettable First Impression

PHILIPPIANS 1:1-2

TODAY'S VERSE

"Paul and Timothy, servants of Christ Jesus, to all the saints in Christ Jesus at Philippi, together with the overseers and deacons: Grace and peace to you from our God and our Father and the Lord Jesus Christ." —Philippians 1:1-2

"5...4...3...2...1...ready or not, here I come!" Kool-Aid-stained fingers pressed into my closed eyelids as friends scurried to hiding places. Desks became castles, chairs became caves, and tapestried drapes became towering fortresses. Squeals filled the air as, one by one, a poorly camouflaged foot or a muffled giggle gave away our secrets. No matter how many times we played Hide and Seek, the game never grew old.

We all walk through seasons when joy plays an unwelcome game of Hide and Seek. Finding joy when life is out of focus can seem daunting. Disappointment, worry, and adversity blur our lens on life, distorting our perspective. This sabotages our ability to experience meaningful relationships and see our potential in Christ. Applying the principles found in Philippians will help us to transform faulty thought patterns and choose contentment regardless of circumstance.

Joy-thirsty women, when life is unraveling, we can find joy by focusing our lens on God's perspective. I encourage you to read the entire book of Philippians before you begin this study.

Paul's lens on life was crafted in the crucible of adversity. The author of Philippians suffered many challenges that could have easily obscured his joy. Over the course of his lifetime, he experienced hardships, blindness, beatings, and imprisonment. Yet, Paul's struggles proved to strengthen his relationship with God.

Paul wrote Philippians while he was under house arrest in Rome c. 61 AD to the church in Philippi, a city named after King Philip of Macedonia, the father of Alexander the Great. Philippi was a prosperous colony of Roman citizens, many of whom spoke Latin and were retired military men.

AMPLIFY

I confess that I tend to ignore or rush through the first few verses of Paul's letters in the New Testament. At first glance, they seem like nothing more than meaningless introductions. In retrospect, it is easy to see how these significant verses set the tone for the rest of the letter. Paul makes an unforgettable first impression.

The beginning of Philippians is typical of Paul's letters. It quickly identifies three elements: the sender, the receiver, and the greeting. Paul and Timothy are working together not as co-authors but as servants of Christ.

How does Paul introduce himself?

_____

_____

I've introduced myself to a lot of people in a lot of places but have never led with, "Hi, I'm Angela, a servant of Christ." Usually, in attempts to make a great first impression, we add a few descriptive titles after saying hello. Paul instantly identifies himself with Christ, making a strong and memorable first impression. His humility challenges me to pull back the tapestried drapes of my life and let you see some seasons when my joy went into hiding. As we begin, allow me to introduce myself as a joy-thirsty girl with a grateful heart.

APPLY

A CALL TO MINISTRY

Growing up, the sound of 88 keys on a piano and voices in three-part harmony often filled our home. Not surprisingly, I majored in Music Education at Evangel University in Springfield, Missouri. I met my husband, Dale Donadio, there while he was studying Pre-Law. After a God-directed shift, he completed his Masters of Divinity in 1993 and we were married a week later. Dale and I spent a year in ministry in Maui, Hawaii, before moving to Virginia, to serve as Youth Pastor and Worship Pastor. These formative years allowed us the opportunity to cut our teeth in ministry before answering the call to serve as Lead Pastors. During nearly two decades of ministry, my relationship with the Lord dramatically changed.

FEARFULLY AND WONDERFULLY MADE

In 2001, my life was deteriorating in every way—body, mind, and spirit. Perfectionism, performance, and the weight of other people's expectations blurred my lens on life. I became aware of how much I found my identity as a person and in Christ in what I did for Him. God was beginning the process of focusing my lens on His perspective, leading me toward a new kind of life. Looking back, I can see how God was lovingly reshaping me, but at the time, it was painful.

For as long as I can remember, I have struggled with physical challenges. As a child, I needed hospitalization for osteomyelitis, a rare condition where the strep virus enters the blood stream, attacking the bone marrow. As I grew older, I faced other complications with my tonsils, my knee, deteriorating eyesight, endometriosis, and a difficult pregnancy resulting in a C-section. Due to endometriosis, I faced a slim chance of ever having children. Despite the doctor's prognosis, I am the blessed mother of two children—my daughter, Gabrielle, born in 1996, and my son, Christian, born in 1999.

I used to refer to myself as "the reject off the assembly line of heaven." Looking at life through the blurry lens of health complications, I didn't like what I saw. However, God convicted me and showed me through His Word, especially through Psalm 139, that I am His design and He has a purpose for me. The words of Psalm 139:14 leapt off the

3

page, "I praise You because I am fearfully and wonderfully made." I had no idea how much I would need that perspective shift.

A DEFINING MOMENT

In 2001, after living with chronic pain from endometriosis, I had a hysterectomy. One week after surgery, I was bleeding badly enough at home to call my doctor. After following his advice and going to the emergency room, they admitted me for observation. To make a long story short, over the course of twelve hours, while fully awake, I lost over half of my blood. Nurses frantically came in and out of my hospital room attempting to stop me from hemorrhaging to death. At 3:30 AM, I looked at the clock and terror became my bedside visitor. I thought to myself, "I'm not going to make it until 6:00 AM when my doctor is on call." That proved to be a defining moment in my life. God was refocusing my lens.

Later, as I was still processing all that had happened, I said to the Lord, "I don't ever want to feel that desperate again." I heard Him respond, "That is how I always want you to feel—that dependent on Me." God was changing the faulty thought patterns that threatened to choke out my joy. I "died" to self in that hospital in a tangible way. I began to journal during this period of my life and my relationship with the Lord became much more intimate and personal. My thoughts and questions became songs that eventually formed my first album, "This Journey." I've included lyrics from the album throughout this study, praying they will inspire you to learn to live in joy no matter where your journey takes you.

We can find joy during seasons of adversity with one subtle shift: allowing God to focus our lens on His perspective. In the coming weeks, we'll see that Paul developed a kingdom perspective, viewing people and circumstances through God's eyes.

Philippians may only be four short chapters long, but don't let that fool you. It's a treasure trove of insights. As we walk through Philippians, we'll discover how we, just like Paul, can find joy during adversity. Get ready for an amazing journey.

ASK

Paul makes an unforgettable first impression. How do you usually introduce yourself and in what way are you inspired by Paul?

_____

_____

What is one area of your life God is challenging you to become more dependent on Him?

_____

_____

Prayer Challenge: _Holy Spirit, open my eyes! I want my first impressions and opening remarks to identify me as a servant of Christ. I want to live a life marked by joy. Help me to understand all that will mean. Amen!_

Behind the Tapestried Drapes

"Come on in!" How I wish I were answering a knock at my door, welcoming you into my home. I'd invite you to choose your favorite mug or cup and saucer from a collection that has overtaken an entire cabinet. We'd sip tea or coffee as we shared stories and perhaps a few tears. I'd savor every moment. Yet, perhaps like me, you've hosted a visitor you never invited. He doesn't call ahead, overstays his welcome, and threatens to unravel our beautiful, tapestried drapes. His name is adversity and his intimidating presence can certainly send our joy into hiding. Yet, adversity can also serve as our teacher, if we allow God to use it to focus our lens on His perspective.

I learned some tough lessons from adversity, and many of them served as the catalyst for this study. Although I'd much prefer sitting with you face to face, please allow me to share my heart with you today. Two difficult seasons of illness nearly pulled apart the fabric of my life. Joy can disappear when health problems, strained relationships, and financial difficulties pay us a visit. No matter what you're facing today, God can give you the strength to persevere and love the life you see.

APPLY

HERE I AM TO WORSHIP

In 2003, I began to feel ill and experience sharp pain I had never known before. I had no appetite and struggled for several months, losing weight and enduring bouts of excruciating pain. After weeks of doctor visits, I was admitted to the hospital. My heart rate had plummeted to 41 beats per minute and my blood pressure was hovering dangerously low at 76/40. I spent eleven days in the hospital with nothing to eat or drink until the doctors scheduled an extensive MRI.

Lying on my side in the only position my body could tolerate, completely alone, I watched the screen as the barium reached my stomach and stopped. The forty-five-minute GI test took seven hours. I lay on the cold, metal table hour after hour—drink, sit up, roll over, stand up, lay down, drink—and I heard the Lord say to me, "Angela, I know you can worship me in the sanctuary. I want to know if you can worship me here." I have led worship hundreds of times, but this hospital room became holy ground. I sang quietly with tears flowing down my face, *"Here I am to worship. Here I am to bow down. Here I am to say that You're my God."* That moment of surrender ushered in my miracle.

There are no coincidences in God. A doctor on call at the hospital saw my films and happened to be studying for his medical board exams. He remembered a picture that looked like my films. They called in more specialists and finally gave me a diagnosis at 7:00 AM the next morning—Superior Mesenteric Artery Syndrome. SMA Syndrome is a rare, life-threatening disorder where the superior mesentery artery takes too sharp a right turn. The first portion of my intestines, my duodenum, was compressing the artery and acting as an obstruction. A severely compressed artery kept my stomach from emptying properly. Two days later, a team of specialists made the decision to perform a duodenal jejunostomy to bypass the affected portion of my intestines and relieve pressure on the artery. Then, they would reconnect the stomach to a lower section of the intestines.

The day of surgery was my low point. We didn't know if I would make it. I remember asking God, "What else could I need to learn? Why is this happening to me?" God reassured that this did not take Him by surprise. I survived the surgery, and after one more long and difficult week in the hospital, I could go home. I spent months reeling from trauma, adjusting to a scar than ran the length of my torso, and unable to eat solid food. Even in those dark days, God was whispering to me, breathing hope into my withered spirit. While recuperating, I took out a piece of paper and scribbled these words:

"I don't understand how this is in Your plan but I'll trust You anyhow. I can't possibly see what good is there for me but I'll trust You anyhow."

This song completed my first album. This became a new way of living for me; learning to trust God's character completely, even when life is out of focus.

A WALK OF FAITH

Following surgery, there were times I questioned why God would spare my life when I couldn't eat or take care of my children the way I desired. He would reassure me that He was with me. His Spirit would remind me, "Because if it's for My glory, it's for your good." I stopped asking God why. Now, I choose to believe that nothing happens to me that isn't filtered first through the loving hands of my Heavenly Father. If you have to know why, you'll never know peace. God won't allow anything to happen to us that He won't use to bring glory for Himself. God will not waste anything you go through. He will use the U-turns, detours, and dead ends. He asks us to let go of the reasons, throw our arms around His neck, and take a walk with Him—a walk of faith. The choice is ours. Don't fight the process God is taking you through. Instead, learn to trust His character.

We don't always have control over what happens to us. I've undergone several endoscopies to dilate (stretch) my esophagus and monitor what I eat. When I'm tempted to feel discouraged, I don't allow my mind and spirit to dwell in those feelings. Instead, when difficulties come, I sustain my joy by reminding myself of who God is. **Knowing God's character helps us trust God's heart.**

We tell our children not to talk to or trust strangers. If you don't know God, He is a stranger to you and you won't be able to trust Him in adversity. You will only grow to know God's character as you study His Word and spend time in His presence. Without trust, you won't be able to surrender your life completely to Christ.

The Bible is full of examples of men and women who faced tremendous adversity and kept their eyes and spirit fixed on the character of God. One of those amazing people is Paul. He wrote over one-third of the New Testament, including the book we are about to study together. The words of this book will guide us to finding joy. If the enemy can steal your joy, he can steal your strength and your testimony. The joy of the Lord is your strength. God is altogether trustworthy. Spend time with Him and

His Word until you completely trust Him regardless of your situation or circumstance. We cannot rise and fall based on external circumstances. I pray that as you take the time to read God's Word, allowing it to find its way into the fabric of your heart and life, you will find greater joy and love the life you see. Applying the principles found in Philippians will assist you in holding your ground amid adversity. I'm sending hugs your way as we begin this adventure!

ASK

Perhaps you're experiencing a season where your joy is hiding behind the tapestried drapes of adversity. What is one area you're asking God to refocus your lens?

_____

_____

What part of my testimony affected you the most and why? What could you relate to?

_____

_____

Consider writing this statement in a prominent place to encourage you this week: **If it's for God's glory, it's for my good.** How can God use a U-turn, detour or dead-end in your life to bring glory to Him?

_____

_____

Priority of Prayer

PHILIPPIANS 1:3-5

TODAY'S VERSE

"Paul and Timothy, servants of Christ Jesus, to all the saints in Christ Jesus at Philippi, together with the overseers and deacons: Grace and peace to you from our God and our Father and the Lord Jesus Christ. I thank God every time I remember you. In all my prayers for all of you, I always pray with joy because of your partnership in the Gospel from the first day until now."

—Philippians 1:1-5

Now that you've come to know a little about me and my journey to finding joy, let's dive into all Philippians has to offer a joy-thirsty girl. Today we'll discover one of Paul's secrets to finding joy: the priority of prayer.

AMPLIFY

A THANKFUL HEART

As Philippians opens, we immediately see Paul's heart for the people. He wants them to grow in God's purposes and receive God's blessing for their lives. Paul is separated from the churches he loves while enduring house arrest in Rome. He has learned to depend on God completely during his difficult circumstances.

What two gifts does Paul ask God to extend to his readers?

_____

_____

He tells them that he thanks God every time he remembers them. The word "thank" means *to express gratitude, appreciation, or recognition owing to, because of, through, by virtue of, or on account of.*

How often does Paul say he thanks God for them?

_____

_____

Always is a powerful word. This indicates a passionate, consistent prayer life. Prayer sustains Paul and connects him with God and others. Physically separated from the believers in Philippi, they are still on Paul's mind and in his heart. Examining the verse again, we discover not only does Paul pray for them, he prays with joy. Go ahead and get used to seeing that word. In some form or another, we find joy mentioned in the book of Philippians sixteen times in four short chapters. The theme of joy saturates the book. I pray that by the end of our time together, the Holy Spirit will form a new understanding of this tiny but powerful word.

"Joy" means *pleasure, extreme gladness, delight, elation, rapture, bliss.* Paul expresses joyful thanksgiving for the Philippians in these opening statements. Paul is known for this type of greeting; it is a trademark of his letters. Over the next few weeks together, we will see how three things mark Paul's life: joy, thanksgiving, and a servant's heart.

Paul identifies his relationship with the Philippians as a partnership. He is delighted they are aware of his ministry, praying for him, and partnering with him. They were prayer partners as well as financial partners, providing support for Paul's missionary journeys from the time Paul first came to Philippi until the close of his first Roman imprisonment. He finds joy through partnership, even under house arrest, as he places top priority on prayer.

APPLY

THE TRUTH IN RED LETTERS

The question offended me at first. *"Why would a church put that on their digital sign? On a main road, no less,"* I thought to myself, feeling slightly insulted. In glaring, red, all capital letters, flashed the jarring question: "IS PRAYER A WASTE OF TIME?"

My initial response? *"Of course it's not! Why even ask that question?"* My neck craned backwards to read it again, as if in slow motion. My thoughts became deliberate and the moment grew heavy. *"Is prayer a waste of time?"* I contemplated.

I wanted to dismiss the question right away as nothing more than a blatant attempt to garner curiosity. I wanted to bellow a resounding *"No!"* to the query. I *wanted* to retort with a mountain of evidence, piled high from the stacks of prayers I've lifted lately. But honesty began to seep in, bleeding onto the page of my well-wishes. If truth be told, my prayer life is sometimes a little lackluster. Okay, maybe a *lot* lackluster. I could make so many excuses. Yet, staring me in the face, in flashing neon lights, was the truth.

I want—desperately—to make my case for the priority of prayer. But my actions often betray me. If I really believe in the power of prayer, why don't I live what I believe? Could I, *horror of horrors*, actually harbor the dangerous notion that prayer is a waste of time?

I know, beyond any doubt, that prayer changes people and prayer changes things. Prayer is my lifeline, my means of communicating with God. Prayer repositions my heart and refocuses my attitudes. Prayer energizes my spirit and gives me renewed purpose. Prayer allows me to hear the heart of my Father for my life and the lives of those I love. Prayer gives me God's perspective and provides divine solutions for situations I'm facing. I can make my case for the importance of prayer. But if all of that is true, and I know it is, why isn't it my highest priority?

Maybe it's because I think I can figure things out on my own.

Maybe it's because I think my time is better spent doing something else.

Maybe it's because I don't think my prayer is really making a difference.

Whatever the reason, and maybe it's all the above and more, it won't change unless I'm honest with myself. It's painful to acknowledge that I needed those bold, red letters. I needed a wake-up call. I needed the reminder that *I can't figure things out on my own...that my time is best spent in prayer...and my prayers really do make a difference.*

Can we ask God to shine His flashlight into any crevices of our hearts where selfishness and doubt crowd out our dependency on Him? After all, prayer is admitting we are completely dependent on God.

Perhaps you also needed the truth in red letters today. Perhaps difficulty has dampened your prayer life or pride has kept you from admitting your dependence on God. If so, hang on to this one thing: **no time you ever spend in prayer is wasted.**

ASK

Paul put a high premium on prayer. What adjustments do you need to make in your attitude and schedule to make prayer a priority?

_____

_____

Have you ever prayed that God would extend His grace and peace to someone? If so, who was it and under what conditions?

_____

_____

How does it make you feel when you know that someone is praying for you?

_____

_____

Prayer Challenge: *I want to do whatever it takes to make prayer a priority in my life. Help me cultivate the desire and devote the time to prayer, study, listening and learning how to pray.*

God's Waiting Room

PHILIPPIANS 1:6-8

TODAY'S VERSE

"Being confident of this, that He who began a good work in you will carry it on to completion until the day of Christ Jesus. It is right for me to feel this way about you since I have you in my heart; for whether I am in chains or defending and confirming the Gospel, all of you share in God's grace with me. God can testify how I long for all of you with the affection of Christ Jesus."
—Philippians 1:6-8

AMPLIFY

Yesterday, we saw how Paul rejoiced in the work God is doing in the church in Philippi. Paul loves seeing not only what God has done for them, but also what He has done *in* them. He is confident that the God who inaugurates is the God who completes. As I write this, I am thinking of so many beautiful women who are in the "waiting room of God." They have seen God begin a work in them or in those they love; however, they have yet to see it completed. Perhaps you know your way around the waiting room of God all too well. Although waiting is challenging, **a delayed destiny doesn't have to derail us.**

CONFIDENT OF THIS

Consider Paul's choice of words in Philippians 1:6—"confident of this."

Is there an area of your life or a person you are praying for that is somewhere between "began a good work" and "carry it on to completion"? If so, describe your feelings and beliefs about God during this time.

_____

_____

Is "confident of this" a part of your description? If not, why?

_____

_____

Let's be honest. **It can be difficult to be confident in God when we're stuck between the promise and the provision.** When the promise seems obscured by circumstances, Jesus' words give us tremendous strength, building up our faith. In Revelation 22:12—13, Jesus describes Himself as the Alpha and Omega, the First and the Last. Alpha is the first letter of the Greek alphabet, and Omega is the last. As an eternal God, He sees the end from the beginning. How do these verses add depth to the passage we are studying today?

_____

_____

He not only sees the end from the beginning, He *is* the beginning and the end. When we commit ourselves to Him and trust Him in all seasons, we can say with confidence that He who has begun a good work will be faithful to complete it!

Let's look at another key statement from Philippians 1:7—"Whether I am in chains or defending and confirming the Gospel."

In this Scripture, Paul lets his readers know that all of them "share in God's grace with me." Not even imprisonment and persecution can change this fact. Shackled and chained to a Roman guard twenty-four hours a day, Paul's spirit was still singing. Paul was enduring tremendous adversity. Finding joy while finding himself in the waiting room of God meant seeking God's perspective and partnering with believers. The Philippians had identified themselves with Paul by sending Epaphroditus as their representative to help and encourage him. They also sent money and gifts. It's one thing for us to identify ourselves with someone when it benefits us. It's another thing altogether to identify with someone whose stand for the Gospel has landed him in prison. He affirms how much their partnership means to him and lets them know how much he loves them and misses them.

CREATED FOR RELATIONSHIP

Part of Paul's source of joy was his relationship with the believers in Philippi, demonstrated by their mutual love and prayer for one another.

In Philippians 1:8, Paul indicates that he doesn't just miss them, he "longs for them" with what?

_____

_____

These verses speak of deep compassion and love. He extends this love to all his readers, impartially and without exception. I can identify with what Paul describes here. I have come to know the joy of partnering in ministry. Part of the calling God has placed on my life is to come alongside pastors and their wives in Africa. When I am at home in the United States, my heart can hardly wait to see the beautiful people in Africa, whom I have come to know and love. I value their prayers for me, and we share in God's grace together as we partner for the Gospel.

God created us for relationship. He did not design us as women to operate in isolation or to serve God in a vacuum. We need others to pray for us and encourage us, especially if we are in a season when waiting can blur our lens on life. Women of God, we desperately need to love and pray for one another rather than hold each other at arm's length. Don't allow hurt or previous disappointments to keep you from soul-strengthening, God-honoring female friendships.

APPLY

Many things can contribute to seasons where we find ourselves in the waiting room of God. Perhaps an illness, the death of a loved one, or a conflict at work has changed the season of your life. As I shared with you when we started our study together, I experienced two life-threatening illnesses in 2001 and 2003. I am familiar with the uncomfortable and frustrating terrain of God's waiting room. Although physical chains or shackles did not confine me, at times my illness felt just as debilitating and restrictive. No matter what is going on around us, including the chains of adversity, the work of God doesn't stop. God is always working, giving us the grace we need for every situation.

ASK

Perhaps you feel like you're in God's waiting room. If so, describe the situation and your feelings and beliefs about God.

Are you cultivating healthy, Godly relationships, or do you struggle in this area? If this is a challenge for you, what is one step you can take to invest in relationships?

_____

_____

Describe how you would like the Holy Spirit to bring change in your life in any areas we have discussed today.

_____

_____

Love that Overflows

PHILIPPIANS 1:9-11

TODAY'S VERSE

> *"And this is my prayer: that your love may abound more and more in knowledge and depth of insight, so that you may be able to discern what is best and may be pure and blameless until the day of Christ, filled with the fruit of righteousness that comes through Jesus Christ to the glory and praise of God."* —Philippians 1:9-11

———————————————

"Wow! Power-packed passage!" Those were the first words I wrote in my journal after reading Philippians 1:9-11. It is so rich with insights to finding joy that we will begin next week's study with these same verses. But let's not get ahead of ourselves...we have plenty to chew on today. By now, you know that Paul wrote this passage to the church at Philippi. However, these verses are also an expression of *God's heart to us*, and then *from us to others*. It's an incredible passage to pray over yourself, your family, and those you meet daily. I committed myself to praying this over my family daily for a year, and it made a real difference in the way I viewed them and walked through everyday life with them.

AMPLIFY

What does Paul pray would grow and overflow?

_____

_____

The word "abound" means *to be plentiful, be rich, teem with or be infested with; prevail, thrive, flourish or be prolific.* To "abound in" means *to be well supplied or furnished with, be crowded with, and be abundant in.* Listen to it this way; "I want your **love** to abound in (be infested with, be well supplied or furnished with, be crowded with, be abundant in) knowledge and depth of insight."

Paul describes genuine love, encouraging us to **love on purpose and love *with* purpose**. When we are intentional about loving God and loving people, our lives demonstrate fruit. It isn't always easy to love this way, which is why we need God to show us how to see people through His eyes. As we allow God to mature us and develop authentic love in us, we are one step closer to finding a life filled with joy.

How does Paul say he wants our love to grow?

_____

_____

As we grow in knowledge of Scripture and God's character, we develop our love relationship with Him. We also expand our ability to view others through His eyes. Knowledge for knowledge's sake doesn't necessarily bring any fruit or compassion. In praying for knowledge and wisdom, we are asking God to equip us with godly discernment, sensitivity, and the ability to love. Why? What is the point?

Reread Philippians 1:10 and write it below:

_____

_____

APPLY

FILLED WITH THE FRUIT OF RIGHTEOUSNESS

When we first moved into our home, we planted my favorite kind of tree, a seedling weeping willow. Today, the regal beauty welcomes me each time I pull into my driveway. Perhaps your first choice would be a stunning dogwood or a fragrant pine. Take a moment and picture today's passage of Scripture as a soaring shade tree, laden with delicious fruit.

Our **roots** are in our commitment to God's process as He shapes us into His image and refocuses our lens. I'm thrilled you're taking the time to invest in yourself and your relationship with Christ by digging into this study. You are gaining knowledge and depth of insight, and you will see fruit because of it!

The **trunk** of this tree is love.

Read 1 Corinthians 13 and list a few characteristics of authentic love.

_____

_____

Which one challenges you the most and why?

_____

_____

The branches, foliage, and produce are the **fruit** of the process.

In today's verse, Paul gives us "fruits" that come from this kind of godly love abounding in our lives:

- Discerning what is best
- Filled with righteousness
- Blameless

What would you end up with if you put all this fruit in a basket? A life that displays the character of God and overflows with joy. God wants us to be blameless and filled with the fruit of righteousness. You might be saying to yourself right now, "Well, I should just stop this study here because I'll never be blameless or righteous." Before you do, please read Philippians 1:11.

How does this Scripture tell us that the fruit of righteousness and the character of God comes into our lives?

_____

_____

Ahhhh...breathe a big sigh of relief! The power to live a blameless life filled with righteousness comes through Jesus Christ. When we surrender our lives to Him and accept Him as our Lord and Savior, He clothes us with His righteousness and gives us the Holy Spirit to grow us in His character. If you have never accepted Christ as your personal

Savior, dear friend, please do that right now. He is standing with arms wide open, ready to take your sin and pain. He gives life, peace, joy, and authentic love through relationship with Him. As I write this, my heart beats with anticipation that you will come to accept the grace and discover the new life Christ offers to you. God loves and values you!

My prayer for you today is Paul's words, "That your love would abound more and more in knowledge and depth of insight so that you may be able to discern what is best and may be blameless until the day of Christ, filled with the fruit of righteousness that comes through Jesus Christ to the glory of praise and God!"

ASK

Would you describe your current walk with God as "growing in love" or "stagnant"? Why did you answer the way you did?

_____

_____

Are you making the best and wisest use of your time, schedule and energies? If not, where might you need greater discernment to implement changes?

_____

_____

Group Study: Write any questions you have from this week's homework to present in class if time allows for you to do so.

_____

_____

Prayer Challenge: *Holy Spirit, I recognize that as love grows in my heart, purity and holiness increase in my life. Let Your love abound in me. I want to overflow and be filled with Your love. Let Your love invade, take over, pervade, swarm over and produce the sweetness of Your character in my life. I want the pervading truth in my life to be love that abounds and a heart that reflects You. Amen.*

"TRUST YOU ANYHOW" / Music and Lyrics by Angela Donadio
From "This Journey"

You think I'd know by now to trust You...

Take a leap of faith, pray for a miracle
Lean on the everlasting arms
Seem like simple words I've said a thousand times
When I was miles away from harm,
But now I'm standing toe to toe
And face to face with what I know
Is much bigger than me, and,

(Chorus)
I don't understand how this is in Your plan
But I'll trust You anyhow, and,
I can't possibly see what good is meant for me
But I'll trust You anyhow

Help me to believe the plans You made for me
Before I ever spoke Your name
And nothing happens now that You don't know about
Your love will always stay the same,
But I can't figure all this out
Don't wanna wrestle with this doubt
So I'm coming to You, 'cause

(Chorus)
I don't understand how this is in Your plan
But I'll trust You anyhow, and,
I can't possibly see what good is meant for me
But I'll trust You anyhow

(Bridge)
And I'll praise You
For I am fearfully and wonderfully made
And remember that You always find a way
To use even the darkest night
To show who You are, so show me...I wanna know who You are

"This Journey" Available on www.angeladonadio.com and iTunes

Session 2

Rejoice by Choice

JOY IN SURRENDER
PHILIPPIANS CHAPTER 1

Filled With Fruit

PHILIPPIANS 1:9-11

TODAY'S VERSE

"And this is my prayer: that your love may abound more and more in knowledge and depth of insight, so that you may be able to discern what is best and may be pure and blameless until the day of Christ, filled with the fruit of righteousness that comes through Jesus Christ to the glory and praise of God." —Philippians 1:9-11

In the summer of 2013, we spent our vacation resting and refreshing on the beaches of the South Carolina coast. On the last day, while I sat peacefully in my green lounger, umbrella overhead and intriguing book in hand, a little girl stole my attention. Her squeals of delight filled the ocean air, captivating my heart. I watched as her tiny frame attempted to tackle the waves licking the shore. Placing her fingers securely around her pint-size board, she ventured into the ocean, a few more feet each time, armed only with the hope of riding in on a wave.

Several joyous minutes passed before Mom, Dad and baby brother waded into the ocean to join her. Distracted by Mom's fabulous bubble-gum pink swimsuit, it took me a minute to notice that, unlike his sister, the little boy wanted nothing to do with the waves. I observed as Dad patiently encouraged him to try to catch one. Unable to be persuaded, Dad's teary son was gently passed to Mom's waiting arms. Dad turned his focus to his daughter and picked her up briskly.

Against the expansive horizon and endless sea, she looked like a toy doll. Dad carried her out to meet wave after crashing wave as she held tight to her board. She was giddy with expectation as Dad held her safely, walking her well past the places where she could swim on her own. "Fearless," I thought to myself. Dad waited until the time was right before turning toward the shoreline. With a giant shove, he pushed her onto the crest of the oncoming wave. She was flying, and for a moment, I was too. Helped by my imagination, her plastic board transformed into a colorful magic carpet, soaring over salted sea.

"Do it again, Daddy!"

I marveled as this beautiful father-daughter dance repeated again and again until the ocean's playground wore her out. Her body may have been tired but her spirit was undaunted. The magic carpet received a much-deserved rest as father and daughter walked triumphantly back to shore.

Safely in her father's arms, board firmly in hand, this brave girl painted a stunning portrait of faith. On my own, I can enjoy the refreshing but shallow waters along the sand. However, when I choose to surrender and trust in my Heavenly Father's strong arms, He picks me up, Bible in hand, and carries me much farther than I would ever dare to go alone. Prompted by His timing and propelled by His grace, I ride the wind of the Spirit in ways I never could have dreamed.

"Do it again, Daddy!" Oh, the joy we find in surrender. We can trust our Heavenly Father to carry us into deeper waters, stronger waves, and a more exhilarating ride with Him. As we begin this week, let me encourage you to surrender your fears and allow Him to pick you up. Trust is an act of surrender. As we embrace surrender, we move one step closer to learning to rejoice by choice.

AMPLIFY

DISCERN WHAT IS BEST

In Philippians 1:9-11, Paul prays that his readers will be able to discern what is best. To "discern" means *to see, perceive clearly with the mind of the senses, visible, apparent, clear, conspicuous, recognizable, and tangible.* Another way to say this is, "I want you to be able to see what is best for you."

Part of finding a life filled with joy is discerning God's best for us. Settling for "good" will rob you of "best." Even good things can carry the unwanted cargo of clutter, draining our emotional, physical and spiritual energies.

List two or three reasons you might be tempted to settle for good instead of best.

_____

_____

_____

_____

We settle when we make choices based on fear rather than faith. If we yield to fear, which does not come from God, we will struggle to surrender to God and discern His best for us. Decisions that find their root in fear produce tainted fruit. When we succumb to fear, faulty thought patterns distort the truth of God's character. What we think forms what we believe, and what *we believe* to be true shapes our decisions. Behind every behavior—constructive or destructive—is a belief.

Let me give you a practical example of this principle in action. Picture a woman in her early 30's who has never married, waiting patiently for a godly spouse. The enemy, poised to exploit her weaknesses and insecurities, preys on her thoughts by feeding her lies. The lies sound something like this:

> *"You will never find a godly spouse. The clock is ticking and no one is going to want you if you get any older. Why are you saving yourself for someone who believes in God? You can meet plenty of great men if you'll just take **that** prerequisite off the table. God doesn't really care that you are lonely, and if He did, He would certainly understand why you need to date a guy that isn't a believer. After all, you can always take him to church and win him to Christ after you get married."*

The enemy tempts us to doubt God's character in the hopes that we will make decisions contrary to God's best. In some cases, we trade in God's best for just plain bad. To discern what is best for us, we need to understand the heart of God. Only when we see ourselves accurately through His Word can we truly accept who we are in Christ. Surrender opens the door for God to refocus our lens as He replaces faulty thought patterns with His truth.

APPLY

FILLED WITH THE FRUIT OF RIGHTEOUSNESS

Once we can discern what is best and surrender to God's plan, we can enjoy one of the rewards of obedience: a life filled with fruit. "Filled" means *to occupy completely, spread over or through, pervade, drill and put a filling into (as in the case of a decayed tooth); crowd, stuff, cram, pack into, abound in, overflow, occupy, take over.* Filled means filled!

In today's passage, Paul describes a life of joy as a life filled with the fruit of righteousness.

What does Galatians 5:22 list as the fruit, or evidence, of the Holy Spirit's work in our lives?

_____

_____

These characteristics are the overflow of righteousness, which literally means *in right standing.* Romans 5 tells us that when we come to Christ, He covers us with the blood of Jesus, clothing us in His righteousness. When God the Father looks at us, He doesn't see us marred by our faults or imperfections. He sees us justified through faith and made righteous through the blood of His Son. One of my favorite names of God is "Jehovah Tsidkenu." It means *God is my righteousness* and translates *to make stiff and straight.*

Ponder that for a moment. **No matter how life may be unraveling, God is providing you with backbone.** He makes things straight and enables you to do the right thing. When righteousness governs our choices, the result is a life characterized by integrity, a genuine concern for others, and the desire to please God. Girlfriends, that is a surrendered life. And a surrendered life is steeped in joy.

ASK

Is there an area where you have traded in God's best for good or just plain bad? If so, confess it to the Lord and ask Him to begin removing every lie the enemy has planted, replacing them with His truth and showing you your value to Him.

_____

_____

_____

_____

How does surrender produce fruit in your life?

_____

_____

If you're facing a decision or situation that requires greater "backbone," take a moment to share that with the Lord, thanking Him for clothing you in His righteousness.

_____

_____

Celebrating Chains

PHILIPPIANS 1:12-14

TODAY'S VERSE

"Now I want you to know, brothers (partners in the faith), that what has happened to me has really served to advance the Gospel. As a result, it has become clear to the whole palace guard and to everyone else that I am in chains for Christ. Because of my chains, most of the brothers in the Lord have been encouraged (become confident) to speak the Word of God more courageously and fearlessly." —Philippians 1:12-14

"Celebrating chains? What kind of title is that?" you might be asking. After all, who in the world celebrates chains? Chains represent a circumstance that is confining or restrictive, and for me, they have come in the form of illness. I've shared honestly about seasons when difficulty blurred my lens on life. While battling illness, I struggled to understand God's plans. I trudged through a myriad of spiritual questions including, "How can I possibly celebrate chains?" It's not that we celebrate the physical or emotional pain that chains bring. We celebrate what God *has done and is doing* through them. Through adversity, we come to know the character of God in ways we might not otherwise experience. God doesn't waste anything we go through. As we surrender every painful situation to Him, He receives glory from working in our lives.

Before we dig into this passage, what past or present chains (i.e., physical, financial, relational, etc.) can you identify in your own life?

_____

_____

AMPLIFY

In Philippians 1:12, Paul describes his suffering by saying, "What has happened to me."

What is Paul referring to? What has happened to him?

_____

_____

Paul says that because of what he has been through, two important things have transpired. What are they?

It has become......

_____

Most of the brothers in the Lord have been......

_____

Paul's joy is unfazed by less than ideal circumstances because he views them through God's perspective. Paul was imprisoned, not because he was guilty of any crime, but because of his stand for the Gospel. If you have grown up in America as I have, it's difficult to grasp the reality that Christians face severe persecution all over the world. In Paul's case, the whole palace guard knows why he is enduring persecution, potentially heightening the danger of his imprisonment.

WHOLE PALACE GUARD

Philippians 1:13 tells us it has become clear to the "whole palace guard" that Paul is in chains for Christ. Why is this significant as we study this passage? The whole palace guard is a contingent of Roman soldiers numbering several thousand, many of whom had personal contact with Paul. During Paul's life, he experienced multiple imprisonments in a variety of environments, including some of the worst dungeons and prisons of his day. While writing Philippians, Paul was under house arrest.

He could visit freely with others while chained to a Roman guard twenty-four hours a day. Guards would rotate shifts, taking four-hour intervals.[1]

Not to overstate the obvious but Paul said he continued to share the Gospel while in chains! Try to put yourself in his position. What might it feel like to spend your days with chains on your wrists and ankles, all the while tethered to a guard? List any potential hardships or complications you think this might cause.

_____

_____

While visiting in Ghana, West Africa, I toured Elmina and Cape Coast Castles, centers of the West African Coast slave trade. I saw the types of cumbersome, iron chains Paul would have worn. I imagine his swollen, bruised hands, lovingly writing to his precious church. I picture his sore legs, aching from stiff joints and restricted movement. Yet, Paul never allowed his shackles to define his outlook.

Look at Verse 14 of today's passage. Paul tells us that what has happened to him has served to do something amazing. What is it?

_____

_____

Paul is hardly maintaining a low profile even though the whole palace guard knows why Paul is in prison. Sharing the Gospel is what landed him there in the first place. The guards, as well as other people in the area, got an up close and personal look at Paul's life and witnessed his unwavering joy.

What do people see—especially non-believers—see when they get an up close and personal look at you?

_____

_____

Something is conspicuously absent from this passage. What Paul doesn't express is almost as important as what he does. Paul is facing injustice, false charges, and iron chains. Yet, we are not reading words laced with bitterness or anger. Instead, he keeps his lens squarely focused on God's perspective.

If you were in Paul's shoes, what might you be tempted to think, feel or say?

_____

_____

I don't know about you, but my words would quickly become weighed down with complaints, frustration and a whole lotta whining. **Our words will change when our thoughts begin to change**. As we surrender our stubborn will to God's perfect will, He will reveal Himself through difficulty. We'll begin to think and respond like Paul. His chains give him three reasons to celebrate:

- They help to advance the Gospel.
- They highlight his stand for Christ.
- They serve to encourage others to share the Word more courageously and fearlessly.

Paul has the right vertical perspective (between him and God), so he is able to have the right horizontal perspective (between him and others). He realizes that God is using an undeserved, painful, and humiliating situation to encourage others and win the lost.

As his brothers in the Lord see what Paul is enduring, they are motivated to speak the Word of God with even more passion, not to retreat. In Rome, Paul is in real danger of losing his life. He could have gone into hiding but he makes the most of every opportunity to share Christ with others. He wants his church to know that his suffering has not been in vain. This is a portrait of a surrendered life.

APPLY

God specializes in extracting kingdom purpose out of the worst of circumstances. The enemy believes that difficulty will chain you to anger and bitterness. However, when you choose surrender, it releases the potential for difficulty to have the opposite effect. Your testimony during a trial not only causes you to stand out to unbelievers, it encourages Christians. I pray that as you take this study, God will give you the opportunity to share your story of His faithfulness. I also pray that when the enemy tries to use something to harm you, God turns that thing around and brings healing instead. Dear friends, this is how we rejoice by choice.

ASK

Look back at what you identified as chains at the beginning of today's lesson. How could you begin to celebrate what God is doing through the situation? If you can't think of anything to write, ask the Holy Spirit to show you God's perspective. How can God bring healing through your trial?

_____

_____

When you find yourself in a difficult situation, think about your response. What are your typical thoughts and attitudes?

_____

_____

Do your responses line up with God's heart? If not, what adjustments do you need to make in your thought patterns and belief systems?

_____

_____

Prayer Challenge: *Holy Spirit, help me to renew my mind so that I can have a godly perspective. Help my life and testimony to witness to the lost and to encourage other Christians. Strengthen those who are in situations just like Paul, in underground churches, in chains, and in danger of losing their lives for speaking Your Word. Give me a heart to see the Gospel advanced more than anything else. Thank You for using trials in my life to bring me to where I am, and to encourage others. Amen.*

The Main Thing

PHILIPPIANS 1:15-18

TODAY'S VERSE

> "It is true that some preach Christ out of envy and rivalry, but others out of goodwill. The latter do so in love, knowing that I am put here for the defense of the Gospel. The former preach Christ out of selfish ambition, not sincerely, supposing that they can stir up trouble for me while I am in chains. But what does it matter? The important thing is that in every way, whether from false motives or true, Christ is preached. And because of this, I rejoice."   —Philippians 1:15-18

If you're counting, here is our second mention of joy. It's also our first mention of some drama happening behind the scenes. While he is under house arrest, some of the ministers of the Gospel are taking advantage of his situation to gain ground for their own personal ministry. Let's get real—Paul is in the trenches. Yet he rejoices by choice.

AMPLIFY

Some teachers of the day were preaching with wrong or insincere motives out of competition with Paul. They were making his imprisonment more difficult to bear. Paul taught a clear message of grace, in stark opposition to the Judaizers' instruction requiring strict adherence to the law. Truthfully, these people were not just opportunists; they were mean.[2]

Some people can be downright mean. What do you believe drives their behavior?

_____

_____

I would love to tell you I have never encountered mean people in my life, least of all not in the ministry. Unfortunately, jealousy, competition, and insecurity fuel some pretty nasty behavior. Mean people thrive off squashing the dreams of others.

Have you encountered a dream killer in your life? If so, how did you handle it?

_____

_____

Even as the plots of cruel people flourished, Paul rejoiced. Paul faced a critical choice: accept an imperfect Christianity (which still exists today) or accept the consequences of people living without the Gospel. To clarify, these teachers were not preaching heresy; their message was true although their motives were not pure.[3]

What are your thoughts on this statement? "The Gospel has its objectivity and validity apart from those who proclaim it."

_____

_____

Even when mean people muddy the waters, the message is more important than the messenger. Although it's disheartening that fellow Christians sought to add to Paul's difficulties, it did not dampen his joy. In their pride and self-interest, they allowed the enemy to use them to bring hurt and division. What was Paul's response? Look at the end of today's verse, Philippians 1:18.

_____

_____

In other words, "Who cares?" He does not deny their actions or their motives; he is honest and upfront about them. He just refuses to allow them to steal his joy. He keeps his focus and perspective on the main thing, "that Christ is preached." No matter what his opponents attempted, they could never steal his joy.

APPLY

Unfortunately, mean people are still around today, doing mean things and just being plain old mean. **We can't control what others do, but we can control our responses to them**. We can keep them from stealing our joy through the power of the Holy Spirit. Remind yourself, a hundred times a day if you need to, that you will not allow anything to take your joy.

No ministry is perfect because no person is perfect. It saddens me to see how some people's choices have blemished the cause of Christ. When this happens, people often become disillusioned with the Church. Regardless of its flaws and imperfections, Christ died for the Church. He loves the Church and we need to as well. Perhaps a Pastor or someone you held in high esteem disappointed you with what you perceived as ugly motives and selfish ambition. If this has turned you away from Christ or away from relationship with other believers, may I lovingly encourage you to surrender that to the Lord? Don't allow the enemy to steal God's best from you. Ask the Holy Spirit to help you to say, "Who cares?" Girlfriends, let's learn a powerful lesson from Paul and keep the main thing the main thing.

ASK

When we as Christians see another in trouble, especially for the sake of the Gospel, how do we respond?

_____

_____

A competitive spirit keeps us from rejoicing in the success of others. Don't let anything obscure the main thing—that people hear the Gospel. If you have any unresolved hurt from church leaders or fellow believers, take a moment to surrender that to Jesus now. Allow the power of the Holy Spirit to soften your heart, enabling you to extend forgiveness and pray for them moving forward.

_____

_____

Prayer Challenge: _Holy Spirit, help me to release any past hurts from churches and leaders. I don't want to allow anything to steal_ *my joy and keep me from Your best for me. Help me to focus on the Gospel and reaching the lost. I want to keep the main thing the main thing. I thank You that through Your power, I can rejoice, even during adversity. I trust You with my life! Amen.*

It's All Good

PHILIPPIANS 1:18-19

TODAY'S VERSE

"Yes and I will continue to rejoice, for I know that through your prayers and the help given by the Spirit of Jesus Christ, what has happened to me will turn out for my deliverance."
—Philippians 1:18-19

We are only a few short verses into Philippians and we have already clearly seen one thing: we will not just stumble into a life filled with joy. You don't need a Martha Stewart handbook to throw a good old-fashioned pity party. It takes no effort whatsoever to invite bitterness or selfishness over for brunch. However, these notorious bandits will make off with your joy every time. Paul has settled in his heart that external circumstances will not alter his perspective on life. Against all odds, Paul intentionally chooses to rejoice. Did you catch that, girlfriends? He is intentional. He is resolved. This is a powerful pre-requisite to finding and keeping your joy.

AMPLIFY

Paul shares two things he knows will carry him through this situation. What are they?

_____

_____

THROUGH YOUR PRAYERS

I love that Paul again stresses how important and valuable their partnership in prayer is to him. Throughout his books, Paul tells his readers that he prays for them, and he asks them to continue praying for him. The tone for this chapter was set in verse 3 when Paul said, *"I pray for you and thank God for you. I pray with joy because of your partnership with me!"* Prayer is Paul's lifeline. **Prayer should be our first defense, not our last resort.**

List two specific ways you could implement positive changes in your prayer life.

_____

_____

HELP GIVEN BY THE SPIRIT OF CHRIST JESUS

The Spirit of Christ Jesus is the Holy Spirit, the Spirit of God the Father.

What do the following Scriptures teach us about the Spirit of God the Father?

Romans 8:9

_____

_____

1 Corinthians 2:10-14

_____

_____

Romans Chapter 8 says if the Spirit of God lives in us, He controls us. 1 Corinthians 2:10-11 says God reveals His will to us by His Spirit. The Spirit of God is also the Spirit of Christ, the second person of the Trinity. John 15:26 says, "When the Counselor (*the Holy Spirit*) comes, whom I (*Jesus*) will send to you from the Father, the Spirit of Truth who gives out from the Father, He will testify about Me (*Jesus*)."

The Holy Spirit functions as our "Paraclete," which means *to come alongside*. The Bible teaches us that He points people to the truth of Jesus Christ. He is our Helper, Advocate, Comforter, Guide, and Intercessor, just to name a few of His many attributes. To "help" means *to provide with the means toward what is needed or sought; to contribute toward alleviating, prevent or remedy, assist, support and be useful, relieve, cure, balm.* The Holy Spirit helped Paul to live in joy and bear up under loneliness and adversity.

He also aided Paul in distinguishing God's direction because Paul was sensitive to His voice. Do you ever wonder how you can know the will of God? I have many times! Here's the good news; we can find those answers in His Word. We can discern His will by spending time in His presence, listening to His Spirit and obeying what He tells us to do.

What does the help of the Holy Spirit mean to you?

_____

_____

TURN OUT FOR MY DELIVERANCE

Paul continuously depends on the power of the Holy Spirit to focus his lens on life. He is confident that this trial will turn out for his deliverance in one of two ways. Either it will end with his release from prison, or it will end in his death, which for him means eternity with Christ. If you amplify today's verse, it reads like this:

> *"I know (have confidence, have in the mind, have learned, able to recall, understand, comprehend, and be acquainted with) that through your prayers and the help (coming alongside me) of the Holy Spirit, I will be delivered!"*

Ultimately, Paul is saying,

> *"It's all good. No matter what, this thing is going to turn out okay. My hope is in the Lord and His purposes and plans for me. My mind is fixed on Him."*

APPLY

We have received God's Spirit so we can understand His Word and have the mind of Christ. God wants us to experience the full potential of His will for our lives, fixing our minds on Him so we can live in perfect peace. Peace is an elusive, sought after commodity that can't be bought or sold. Isaiah 26:3 reveals how we can find this powerful gift. Write this Scripture below:

_____

_____

The key to peace is fixing our minds on Christ and His purposes. This Scripture doesn't tell us God will keep us out of trials, but in and at peace no matter what is going on around us. Our mindset frames our perspective. What we believe about God will dictate our choices. Picture your mindset as a radio station dial, constantly scrolling through frequencies. When adversity knocks, we might be tempted to stop on fear, confusion, or anger. The same Holy Spirit that sustained Paul renews our mind through Scripture and tunes the frequency to joy.

Perhaps a trial has set the frequency of your mind to anxiety. The Holy Spirit is coming alongside you today, enabling you to know God's heart in every situation. We can tune our mindset to joy by surrendering to God's perfect will. Let's move one step closer to finding a life of joy by echoing Paul's words:

"It's all good. No matter what, this thing is going to turn out okay. My hope is in the Lord and His purposes and plans for me. My mind is fixed on Him."

ASK

Are you confident about God's plans for your life? Why or why not?

_____

_____

Is any area of your mindset stuck on the wrong frequency? If so, surrender it to the Holy Spirit and ask Him to tune the frequency to joy.

_____

_____

Prayer Challenge: *Lord, I need to have my mindset continually renewed by You. I need You to fill me with joy and enable me to keep my focus on Christ. Help me to be more disciplined in prayer. Thank you for prayer partners, those who pray for me, and help me to be that for others! Amen.*

Clothing Yourself with Courage

PHILIPPIANS 1:20

TODAY'S VERSE

"I eagerly expect and hope that I will in no way be ashamed, but will have sufficient courage so that now as always Christ will be exalted in my body, whether by life or by death." —Philippians 1:20

Paul finds his joy in one thing. Wanna take a guess? More than anything, Paul wants Christ to be exalted; his source of joy is Christ.

We might be tempted to think of Paul as superhuman, able to leap tall buildings in a single bound. This is dangerous, because it risks putting Paul on an unattainable pedestal, making a faith-filled, Spirit-controlled life seem unrealistic for any of us in the real world. Let's not entertain that lie from the enemy for one second. Paul was flesh and bone, just like us. He lived an extraordinary life as he depended fully on the power of the Holy Spirit and surrendered completely to his Heavenly Father.

My study Bible adds this: "Circumstances of imprisonment, with all its attendant suffering and oppression, constitute a real temptation for Paul to abandon the Gospel and his resolute service for Christ." God worked in and through Paul to give him grace, insight, discernment, and the attitude/mind of Christ.[4]

Is there any circumstance or situation in your life right now that is causing you real temptation to abandon the Gospel? If so, confess it to the Lord and ask Him for the grace and power to overcome the enemy's efforts to derail your life and testimony.

AMPLIFY

Paul's words are infused with full confidence in God. Circle words that reinforce this.

> *"I eagerly expect and hope that I will in no way be ashamed, but will have sufficient courage so that now as always Christ will be exalted in my body, whether by life or by death." —Philippians 1:20*

Let's look at some of these faith-filled words and phrases that help us develop God-confidence.

EAGERLY EXPECT

Paul does not just say he expects, but he adds that he eagerly expects. When we pray, it is important to pray with expectancy, trusting God to hear and respond to our prayers. "Expect" means *to look forward to, foresee, envision, anticipate, watch or look for, wait for, want, require, need.*

Which of these might Paul be expecting?

- I'm getting these chains off today.
- I won't be ashamed.
- This is the last time I will experience struggle or trial.
- I will have sufficient courage for whatever lies ahead.

Not only does Paul enthusiastically expect God to be his source of strength and joy, he puts his hope in God. Hope is expectation and desire combined. You can lose your purse, your keys and even your wallet, and life will return to normal relatively quickly. However, if you lose hope, life plods along, carrying the baggage of a burdened soul. With Paul's hope firmly fixed on Christ Jesus, he knows no matter what happens to him, Christ will be magnified.

IN NO WAY BE ASHAMED

Paul's difficulty is on display, which let me just say, is no small thing. When we are enduring a challenging season, it is hard enough without social media and gossipers making it everyone's business. When our children disobey, our credit card comes back declined, or our favorite pair of pants will not go past our hips, our instinct is to climb into the nearest hole. Paul stands his ground, determined not to let adversity cover him in shame. He is confident that, with God's help, he will not fail, lose his testimony, or suffer humiliation. He passionately counts on God's grace to keep him from losing heart. Come on girls; scramble out of those hiding places and **clothe yourself with courage.**

BUT...I WILL HAVE SUFFICIENT COURAGE

"But"—I love seeing this three-letter word in Scripture. It serves as a crossroads between two paths. Instead of being ashamed, humiliated, and afraid, Paul states, "I will have sufficient courage." What is interesting is that he says "sufficient" courage—enough courage. God wants us to stay in a place of surrender, dependent on Him. As we learn to trust Him completely as our source, He will give us enough courage for each situation.

In what way do you need His courage today?

_____

_____

Today's verse, Philippians 1:20, contains the purpose of Paul's existence: "So that Christ will be exalted in my body." We have already seen his attitude: his focus is on the Gospel and his mind is on Christ. He is able to say to his readers, "Even if death awaits me, why should now be any different? Why should these circumstances cause me to waver?" He trusts in the power of Christ to work in him and sustain him. He has completely surrendered his life to Jesus Christ, the source of his joy. He lives for one purpose: to exalt Christ.

APPLY

Allow me to take you back with me to Mary Washington Hospital in October of 2003. The sobering moments leading up to surgery left deep imprints on my mind. I can still feel the wheels of the gurney turning as it carried me to the operating room. I can hear the concern in my husband and parents' voices as they lifted tearful prayers. I can sense the awkward tension in the air as I attempted to joke with the surgeon. I can remember the haunting question that turned itself over and over in my mind: *would I see my children again?* Mustering up the courage to face this giant was no small feat.

Courage is not the absence of fear. It is the ability to disregard fear, demonstrating bravery and dauntlessness. Paul had genuine cause for fear. He knew there was a real possibility he might die at the hands of the Romans. He did not deny it; he embraced it and surrendered it by putting it under the covering of God's character.

ASK

Describe an event in your past or present which required you to clothe yourself with courage. Resist the temptation to minimize your situation. Identify, if you can, what steps you took to muster the ability to disregard fear.

_____

_____

What do you need to put under the covering of God's character? Add to the list I have started...

God's Character
"What If's" ... Fear ... Losing my health ...

_____

_____

If you could have a conversation with Paul today, what would you share with him as your greatest takeaway from your study so far?

_____

_____

Prayer Challenge: *Lord, I purpose that You will be exalted in my life. I believe and trust You that I will not be afraid or ashamed. You will give me sufficient courage for whatever I face in life. I thank You that Your Word says Your grace is sufficient for me and Your power is made perfect in my weakness. Amen.*

"JOY" / by Jessie Laine Powell
From "It's a New Day"

Joy, Joy, Joy, I've got Joy...

I've got a beautiful life
I could complain but I am grateful for the simple pleasures
Bills are paid, I'm alive and well today
Tomorrow is not promised, for today I will say I've got

Joy....

I've got a wonderful life
When I go to bed I can rest my head from the daily pressures
My family and friends they care for me
Tomorrow is not promised, for today I will say I've got

Joy...

(Bridge)
No matter what may come
No matter what may go
No matter what's ahead
No matter what's been said
No matter what they do
I can rely on You
The joy of the Lord is my strength,
burning deep within me
I've got joy

Tomorrow is not promised, for today I will say
Joy

"It's A New Day" Available at www.angeladonadio.com and iTunes

— Session 3 —

Perspective is Everything

JOY IN RELATIONSHIP
PHILIPPIANS CHAPTER 1

DAY 1 / MOST PRIZED POSSESSION—CH 1:21

DAY 2 / YOUR CHOICES MATTER—CH 1:22-24

DAY 3 / OVERDRAWN OR OVERFLOWING?—CH 1:25-26

DAY 4 / ON YOUR BEST BEHAVIOR—CH 1:27-28

DAY 5 / GRANTED SUFFERING—CH 1:29

Most Prized Possession

PHILIPPIANS 1:21

TODAY'S VERSE

"For to me, to live is Christ and to die is gain." —Philippians 1:21

I am not a morning person. Rolling out of bed while it is still eerily dark constitutes a small miracle. Nonetheless, while in Phoenix, Arizona for a women's conference, I was highly motivated to set my alarm for— *yawn*—4AM. The night before, I had spotted a brochure in the hotel lobby advertising a glorious way to experience the Sonoran Desert. I couldn't resist the opportunity to do something I had dreamed about for two decades. With the lure of freshly brewed coffee and the promise of adventure, I managed to persuade my dear friend Tracy to join me. Throwing caution and common sense to the wind, we headed out, a la Thelma and Louise, to enjoy an exhilarating ride aboard a hot air balloon.

We arrived at the launch site to discover our brightly colored balloon stretched out over the desert floor. After giving us a few safety tips, our guides began inflating it using large tanks filled with propane. I have to admit, it was at this moment I wondered if a thin sheet of nylon, shooting flames of fire and a small wicker basket seemed a wise combination, especially considering it was about to be my mode of transportation.

"You only live once," I thought to myself.

I awkwardly threw my leg over the rim and climbed in. We lifted off and took flight, propelled only by fire and wind. Within moments, golden and auburn hues filled the Arizona sky as the sun majestically broke over the mountain ridge. It had been a long time since I had watched a sunrise. *Too* long. Loosely directed by our fearless pilot, we began steadily ascending to 1200 feet until we were soaring in the open air.

Everything looked different. I felt different. I breathed deeply, acutely aware of the silence and serenity I had been missing back on the ground. Flying high above cactus and circumstances, I received an unexpected gift: a transformed perspective.

If the fear of heights—or just plain sanity—scratches a hot air balloon ride off your list, not to worry. Paul's letter to the Philippian church provides ample ground for a new perspective. As we will see, perspective is everything. Today's verse boldly displays Paul's secret to continual joy. His source, and most prized possession, is Jesus Christ.

AMPLIFY

To Paul, even the sting of death is tempered by the gain of eternity with Christ. What do Acts 9 and 1 Timothy 1:12-14 tell us about Paul's life as "Saul"?

_____

_____

In what ways might Paul's past frame his perspective, his relationship with Christ and his desire to see the Gospel advanced?

_____

_____

NO POSSESSION SHOULD POSSESS US

On October 25, 2012, Hurricane Sandy pummeled the Eastern Coast, leaving parts of New York and New Jersey devastated by the storm's unmerciful path. For weeks, people went without electricity and stood in lines to receive rationed gas. I watched as shocked families stood in the ruins of what had been their home. Some were on their hands and knees, digging through charred rubble, painstakingly looking for any remaining item of value. A box of old photos containing an unharmed wedding portrait provided a welcome respite for a grieving wife.

Any of our valued possessions—our homes, pets, or our photos—can be lost in a moment. Physical, emotional, and financial hurricanes are the harsh realities of life. Finding joy in the rubble is possible only when we seek God's perspective. Paul's most prized possession was his relationship with Christ. Even in the eye of the hurricane, he is unwilling to relinquish his faith. He takes it a step further and says, "I don't even place value on my life compared to advancing the kingdom of God. If I live, it is to see the Gospel preached. If I die, it is to be with Christ, and see others will preach the Gospel. Either way, it's a win-win situation." Paul kept his eyes fixed on eternity, which enabled him to make the statement in the verse we are studying today. What is that statement?

_____

_____

APPLY

The danger of becoming too comfortable here on earth is that it can dampen our hunger for heaven.

1 Peter 1:3-7 shares the following:

"Praise be to the God and Father of our Lord Jesus Christ! In his great mercy he has given us new birth into a living hope through the resurrection of Jesus Christ from the dead, and into an inheritance that can never perish, spoil or fade. This inheritance is kept in heaven for you, who through faith are shielded by God's power until the coming of the salvation that is ready to be revealed in the last time. In all this you greatly rejoice, though now for a little while you may have had to suffer grief in all kinds of trials. These have come so that the proven genuineness of your faith—of greater worth than gold, which perishes even though refined by fire—may result in praise, glory and honor when Jesus Christ is revealed."

Through God's mercy, we have new birth into what?

_____

_____

Through faith, we are shielded by what?

_____

_____

Verse 6 contains a word we are starting to become familiar with. "In this you greatly" what?

_____

_____

What is of more worth than gold?

_____

_____

What does this reveal as our most prized possession?

_____

_____

Faith is complete trust or confidence, even without logical proof. It is a certainty or conviction. Trials prove our faith to be genuine and result in glory to God. However, much of that depends on our attitude and obedience in the middle of the hurricane. We can easily fall prey to placing too much value on things that are of temporal importance. In our status-driven society, we can value things above people, including our relationship with Christ. The Value Inventory below takes a close look at our priorities, revealing what really matters to us.

It's understandable that possessions carry value. **Just be careful that possessions don't possess you.** Be honest with yourself. What are three of your most valuable possessions? Perhaps attachment to memories gives something even more sentimental value than monetary worth.

_____

_____

Paul views adversity through the lens of God's perspective, allowing him to see even death as a reward. Girls, this is not our home. When Jesus eclipses everything else of value, heaven becomes a lot easier to see.

ASK

"Possession" means *to take over, have power over, influence, hold, or consume*. With that as a definition, what is the one thing that should have this kind of power in our lives?

_____

_____

What do you value most?

_____

_____

What does the statement, "To live is Christ and to die is gain" mean to you?

_____

_____

Your Choices Matter

PHILIPPIANS 1:22-24

TODAY'S VERSE

> *"If I am to go on living in the body, this will mean fruitful labor for me. Yet what shall I choose? I do not know! I am torn between the two: I desire to depart and be with Christ, which is better by far; but it is more necessary for you that I remain in the body."*
> —Philippians 1:22-24

Chicken or pasta? Black flats or wedge heels? Cut my hair or let it grow?

Choices. Some days, those are the hardest ones we face. Yet some, the real mile-markers in life, can flood us with anxiety. *"Should I take this job? Is this the person God wants me to marry? Will my daughter flourish at this University? Should I have this surgery?"* Significant decisions can suffocate us under the weight of their consequences. In today's verses, we see Paul carrying the burden of life and death choices. His example gives us a roadmap for navigating through life when our choices really matter.

AMPLIFY

FRUITFUL LABOR

Paul stacks up the fruit of his ministry against the promise of heaven and finds himself legitimately torn. The churches he has helped to plant, the co-laborers in the faith and the salvation of members of the palace guard serve as a tremendous blessing to Paul. However, it all pales in comparison to being with Christ.

What is the key phrase in today's passage that indicates his reason or motive for staying on earth? Why does he say it's "more necessary" to remain in the body?

_____

_____

Paul's reason to stay is completely others-minded. He puts the needs of others ahead of his personal needs, comfort, or preference. Having given up his rights, his life was all about Christ and the Gospel.

Is it difficult for you to give up your rights to something? Why or why not?

_____

_____

For Paul, the point of living is to be productive and effective. By this time, Paul had undertaken three major missionary journeys and written most of his letters. We know these letters as books of the New Testament: Thessalonians, Galatians, Corinthians, Ephesians, Colossians, and Philemon. Any modern-day missionary would admire and dream of such accomplishments. Yet, Paul isn't finished. He still senses the call and burden to those he has partnered with in ministry.[5]

Paul completed another missionary journey and wrote 2nd Timothy even after his release from Rome. Paul wants his life to matter. He is telling us as his readers, "If I'm going to be here, I want it to mean something for the kingdom. If I must go through this, extract kingdom purpose."

What are some of the potential challenges and benefits of living an others-minded life?

_____

_____

APPLY

Choose an others-minded life. Viewing our choices through this outlook gives our lives significance and purpose for the kingdom of God. Indicate which of the perspectives below best represents your feelings right now. If none apply, write your feelings in the "Other" space provided. Then, in the second column, write your thoughts about the statement you identified with the most.

✓	I MOST IDENTIFY WITH:	MY THOUGHTS ABOUT THIS ARE:
	Perspective 1: I'm young, newly saved, or an inexperienced Christian, and feel like I haven't even begun to do all God has called me to do for the kingdom of God.	
	Perspective 2: I've spent my life serving God, legitimately torn between "remaining in the body" and packing my bags for heaven.	
	Perspective 3: My best years are behind me. I can't imagine any more use I can be in the kingdom of God.	
	Other	

How I would love to hear your answers and discuss the amazing plans God has for you. Friends, our perspectives affect the choices we make. At this season in my life, I will let you know I chose Perspective

2. If you checked Perspective 3, renounce the lies of the enemy and replace it with the truth of God's Word. Regardless of the reasons you may have identified with this perspective (age, changes or hardships in your ministry, church or job), please know that you are valuable in the kingdom. Your life matters.

ASK

What would your obituary say about you if it was written right now?

_____

_____

What do you want it to say?

_____

_____

Are you truly living an others-minded life? If not, what is stopping you?

_____

_____

⁓

If you are doing nothing, God doesn't need to give you any help in doing nothing. Go out and do something impossible for Jesus, and then God will help you. —Reinhard Bonnke[6]

Overdrawn or Overflowing?

PHILIPPIANS 1:25-26

TODAY'S VERSE

"Convinced of this, I know that I will remain, and I will continue with all of you for your progress and joy in the faith, so that through my being with you again your joy in Jesus Christ will overflow on account of me." —Philippians 1:25-26

Overdrawn. It's a word no one wants to see stamped across their bank statement. Yet far too many women limp through life with "overdrawn" written across their hearts. Events, people, and our responses to them can make withdrawals or deposits in our lives. Our joy doesn't have to be siphoned by adversity. We can keep our heart account full even when withdrawals beg to deplete us. If your joy balance is dangerously low, allow God's Word to replenish you today.

AMPLIFY

CONVINCED OF THIS

In today's verses, we see that Paul is convinced of three things about the church in Philippi:

The people still need him for spiritual growth.

He will continue with them in their progress and joy.

Christ's joy will overflow in them.

Paul's life account is infused with joy and faith, and he wants to deposit it into them. Paul's imprisonment weighed heavily on his readers. Without his presence, the overseers could easily become derailed by discouragement. Even from prison, it's important to Paul to continue depositing into their lives.

APPLY

The best investment you'll ever make isn't in a bank; it's in people. We can't give what we don't have, so our influence depends on our investment in ourselves. We need to intentionally make deposits into our joy account, not just enough to be above a zero balance, but until it overflows. Make a list of some items in your life that might fall into these two categories.

JOY ACCOUNT	
WITHDRAWALS	**DEPOSITS**

Which is a longer list? Is your joy account overdrawn or overflowing?

What area of your life is most desperate for a deposit?

_____

_____

ASK

God wants our joy to overflow so we can become instruments of His peace in the lives of others. What does Luke 6:45 teach about the overflow of the heart? What is overflowing in your life?

_____

_____

Think about the people God has placed in your life: your spouse, children, co-workers, extended family, church members, and others. Is their Joy Account overdrawn or overflowing due to your investment into their lives? Are you making withdrawals or deposits through your influence in their lives?

_____

_____

Which of the following action steps from today's passage challenge you the most and why?

- To bring glory to God
- To spread the Gospel and serve others
- To be committed to their spiritual growth and progress
- To bring joy to others, causing them to overflow in their joy account because of me

_____

_____

Prayer Challenge: *Lord, I want my life to bring glory to You. I want my life to overflow with the fruit of Your Holy Spirit. Let Your joy be in me! Keep me moving forward in You. Thank You for meeting my needs so I can help meet the needs of others. Amen.*

On Your Best Behavior

PHILIPPIANS 1:27-28

TODAY'S VERSE

"Whatever happens, conduct yourselves in a manner worthy of the Gospel of Christ. Then, whether I come and see you or only hear about you in my absence, I will know that you stand firm in one spirit, contending as one man for the faith of the Gospel without being frightened in any way by those who oppose you."

—Philippians 1:27-28

"Sit still. Elbows off the table. Stand up straight. Don't talk with your mouth full." I heard those words more than once growing up, especially when company came for dinner. You could sum up the expectation in one phrase: "I need you to be on your best behavior." Many moms and dads have passed on the same words of encouragement to their children. Today, we'll see Paul strike a parental tone as he guides the church in his absence. His charge is to demonstrate behavior worthy of the Gospel. It's easy to be on my best behavior spiritually if everything's going my way. But when difficulty throws a wrench into my perfectly-laid-plans, I'm tempted to throw a tantrum worthy of a time-out. We don't have to get stuck in the terrible twos. Pull up a chair and join me at the table—elbows allowed!

AMPLIFY

WHATEVER HAPPENS

It's difficult to start a sentence with "whatever happens" without God's perspective. Paul pens these words while he is under attack for his faith. He is unsure of the outcome of his imprisonment, and concerned about how the church in Philippi might react. Paul is emphasizing, "If I die here, keep the faith! Don't lose your testimony through your actions." He acts proactively, asking them to be on their best behavior, no matter what. His words are just as timely for us today. Joy-thirsty women, we need to learn to say, "whatever happens in my career, in my marriage, in my health, in ..., I will trust God."

WORTHY OF THE GOSPEL

Just as a good parent guides their children, our Heavenly Father asks His children to act with integrity. We will experience joy in relationships when we operate in unity. Paul asks his readers to contend as "one man," united in purpose and spirit. "Contending" means *to strive, fight, compete, assert, maintain.* He wants his children to be committed to God and to the Gospel, not just to Paul (or to a man). He knows that the potential for them to resort to anger or division is lurking around the bend. This would break his heart. Unfortunately, when a church or ministry is built around a man or woman, and that leader disappoints, people can be left disillusioned and divided. Paul implores them to remain bold in the face of hostility. He does not sugar coat the reality of opposition for the Gospel. He wants them to anticipate it, pray about it, and be ready to contend in unity.

Based on today's passage, what should the focus of the church be when disappointments arise?

_____

_____

We have access to the Gospel at a great cost: the blood of Jesus Christ. When we ask God for His perspective, we can respond to situations in a way that is worthy of His sacrifice. He enables us to face any challenge, not in our own strength, but empowered by the Holy Spirit.

Evaluate each item in the following list by asking yourself if you are living in a way that is worthy of the Gospel.

The way I speak

_____

_____

The way I treat people

_____

_____

The way I react when life throws a wrench

_____

_____

Let's worry a little less about whether we're talking with our mouths full and a little more about the words filling our mouths. It's much easier to be on our best behavior when we ask God to give us His perspective. He also gives us a spiritual wardrobe and the strength to "stand firm" regardless of the wrench life throws our way.

ASK

Read Ephesians 6:10-20, which shares the wardrobe of the full armor of God.

How do these verses from Ephesians 6 help us to know how to stand firm in the enemy's onslaught?

_____

_____

Which piece of the armor stands out to you most and why?

_____

_____

In your opinion, what is the opposite of standing firm?

_____

_____

⌒

If God sends us on stony paths, we are provided strong shoes.
—Corrie Ten Boom[7]

Granted Suffering

PHILIPPIANS 1:29

TODAY'S VERSE

"For it has been granted to you on behalf of Christ not only to believe on Him, but also to suffer for him, since you are going through the same struggle you saw I had, and now hear that I still have." —Philippians 1:29-30

God always has our best interest at heart. He is not unkind, cruel, or arbitrary. If we have accepted Christ as our Savior, nothing happens to us that is not first filtered through the loving hands of our Heavenly Father. Beautiful sisters, we must keep this in mind when the uninvited guest of suffering visits our door. Before we bolt the lock and pretend we aren't home, let's allow Paul's words to offer fresh perspective on this sticky subject.

AMPLIFY

GRANTED

The people of Philippi were enduring persecution under the Roman Empire and trying to hold onto their faith. Amid opposition, Paul tells his readers that something has been granted to them. What is it?

_____

_____

Granting something to someone is the idea of a *gift or a privilege*. It also means *to consent or fulfill a request or to allow.* My study Bible puts it this way: "Christian suffering, as well as faith, is a blessing. The Christian life is a "not only...but also" proposition.[8]

Look at today's passage and fill in the proposition.

"For it has been granted to you on behalf of Christ **not only to**:

_____

but also to:

_____

Paul is telling them that God has granted them this privilege. How is he paying them a compliment?

_____

_____

The church in Philippi is suffering due to persecution for the Gospel. In what way(s) have you endured suffering for the Gospel, and considering today's passage, how might you view it as a compliment?

_____

_____

SUFFER

The word literally means *to undergo pain, grief, damage; experience or be subjected to pain, loss, grief; agonize, smart, hurt, sweat, ache, deteriorate, diminish, endure, feel, bear, withstand.*

Which three words from the sentence above stand out to you the most? Why did you choose those words?

_____

_____

APPLY

GOING THROUGH THE SAME STRUGGLE

The believers in Philippi went from watching Paul suffer to experiencing suffering first-hand. Joy-thirsty women, watching someone else go through heartbreak and experiencing it ourselves are two entirely different things. First-hand knowledge of suffering can blur our lens on life by providing a platform for resentment. The enemy would love nothing more than to see our faith and testimony crumble under the weight of adversity. **Suffering has the potential to grow a root of bitterness or the fruit of the Spirit.**

If we will choose to seek God's heart, He will strengthen our faith in trials. When we suffer for the Gospel, we are granted the opportunity to know God's character in richer ways, finding the joy only He can give. When we get a glimpse of our situation from heaven's vantage point, we embrace the chance to come alongside someone else going through the same struggle.

What struggle have you come through that you could share to encourage someone else?

_____

_____

God knew we would need encouragement when life is out of focus. The Bible is bursting with stories that reveal the character of God and His promise to bring kingdom purpose out of pain. The books of Job and Ruth give us a male and female perspective on loss, suffering, redemption, and restoration. Peter expresses in 1 Peter 3:14, "But even if you should suffer for what is right, you are blessed." Yet our greatest model of obedience through suffering is Jesus Christ. Hebrews 4:15-16 shares, "For we do not have a high priest who is unable to empathize with our weaknesses, but we have one who has been tempted in every way, just as we are—yet he did not sin. Let us then approach God's throne of grace with confidence, so that we may receive mercy and find grace to help us in our time of need." We aren't alone. No matter what you're going through today, God is with you and He will use your struggle to speak hope to someone else.

It's easy to stage a protest when suffering shows up. Standing for the Gospel will not always be popular or easy. Yet, as we surrender to sovereignty, we experience His faithfulness. Joy-thirsty women, perspective is everything. Let's put our trust in God and begin to love the life we see.

ASK

What have you been able to learn from watching others going through the same struggle?

_____

_____

LOOK DEEPER

Look up the following Scripture references and note what each says about suffering, especially in the context of suffering for the cause of Christ. Which verse stands out the most to you and why?

Matthew 5:11-12

_____

_____

Acts 5:41

_____

_____

James 1:2

_____

_____

1 Peter 4:14

_____

_____

⌐◡⌐

"NAIL-PIERCED HANDS" / Music and Lyrics by Angela Donadio
From "It's A New Day"

Broken, wounded, misunderstood,
Rejected, abandoned, hung on a piece of wood,
The Son of God, the Great I am
Became the substitute for man
And Jesus understands when I'm

Broken, wounded, misunderstood,
Rejected, abandoned, desperate to see the good,
It's in that place You call my name
Tell me again You took my pain
So I can understand;

(Chorus)
It is Your nail-pierced hands that hold me
I know You love me and that gives me strength to stand
It is Your nail-pierced hands that hold me
Your mercy came and drew a line in the sand
With Your nail-pierced hands.

Mended, forgiven, loved as I am
Accepted, reborn, and free to give again
The Son of God, the Great I am
Became the substitute for man
And Jesus understands (Chorus)

(Bridge)
There have been times when I felt devastated, left for dead,
Hopelessly lost and wondering what I'd face in days ahead,
But in those moments when I questioned how I'd make it through,
My hope, my strength, my source, I found it all in You.

(Chorus)
It is Your nail-pierced hands that hold me,
I know You love me and that gives me strength to stand
It is Your nail-pierced hands that hold me
Your mercy came and drew a line in the sand
With Your nail-pierced hands.

"It's A New Day" Available on www.angeladonadio.com and iTunes

— *Session 4* —

Dynamic Duo: Unity and Humility

JOY IN HARMONY
PHILIPPIANS CHAPTER 2

DAY 1 / UNITY—CH 2:1-2

DAY 2 / THE VIP TREATMENT—CH 2:3-4

DAY 3 / A PICTURE OF HUMILITY—CH 2:3-4

DAY 4 / A SERVANT'S ATTITUDE—CH 2:5-8

DAY 5 / A NEW SONG—CH 2:9-11

Unity

PHILIPPIANS 2:1-2

TODAY'S VERSE

"If you have any encouragement from being united with Christ, if any comfort from his love, if any fellowship with the Spirit, if any tenderness and compassion, then make my joy complete by being like-minded, having the same love, being one in spirit and purpose." —Philippians 2:1-2

Batman and Robin. Laurel and Hardy. Mickey and Minnie. Butch Cassidy and the Sundance Kid. We know these dynamic duos for their unique chemistry and universal appeal. This week we will meet the dynamic duo of unity and humility in Philippians Chapter 2. They have a lot to teach us about discovering the joy in harmony.

In Chapter 1, we saw Paul's love and appreciation for the church in Philippi. Now, he shares his deep desire for them to live in unity. Unity is so important to Paul that he tells the church it would make his joy complete to see it realized in their lives. Unity is a critical component to pleasing God and positioning ourselves for blessing. Since God's Word emphasizes the importance of unity, we should make the pursuit of it central in our lives.

AMPLIFY

In today's verse, "united with Christ" can be read as "united in Christ," indicating a personal relationship through salvation. Today we will take important phrases from Chapter 2:1-2 and put them in a list to identify the key points. For example, Paul gives us an "If...Then" proposition in verses 1 and 2.

List the four "If's" Paul mentions in the proposition:

1. If you have any ... _____.
2. If you have any ... _____.
3. If you have any ... _____.
4. If you have any ... _____.

What is the then?

Then: _____.

Paul lists three actions that would bring him joy.

1. Being ... _____.
1. Having the ... _____.
1. Being one in ... _____.

COMFORT FROM HIS LOVE

Knowing God loves us gives us comfort and reassurance. When we put our hope in Christ, we can rest knowing we receive forgiveness of sins and eternal life.

How do the following Scriptures confirm the comfort we have from His love?

Romans 5:8

_____

_____

Romans 8:38-39

_____

_____

FELLOWSHIP WITH HIS SPIRIT

Paul states as fact that his readers are operating in the *If List*, demonstrating genuine compassion and care for one another. He wants them to know that because they are functioning this way, he expects the result to be unity. Notice Paul says unity, not uniformity. "Unity" is the *common disposition to work together and serve one another; to have the attitude of Christ.*

What does Romans 12:16 tell us about what kind of attitude we should have?

_____

_____

APPLY

Paul is urging his readers to consider all the benefits, or amenities, that come from having a relationship with Christ and serving Him: encouragement from salvation, comfort from His love, and fellowship with His Spirit. If you've ever stayed at a hotel, you receive a list of amenities, including anything from free wireless internet, a hair dryer, turndown service and chocolates on your pillow (if you're lucky!). Some people even make hotel selections based on the list of perks. When we consider the blessings that come from a personal relationship with Jesus Christ, a list of hotel conveniences pales in comparison. Paul wants them to remember all they have received as a motivator to live in unity. He puts such a premium on unity that he tells them it would make his joy complete. He wants them—and us—to be like-minded, having the mind-set of Christ. When we do, we will have the same love for one another, and will be one in spirit and purpose.

You may be asking why unity is so important. Does it really make that much of a difference? Look at the following passages of Scripture and identify the result of operating in unity: **Power, Blessing, and a Witness to the Lost.**

> *"All the believers were one in heart and mind. No one claimed that any of their possessions was their own, but they shared everything they had. With great power the apostles continued to testify to the resurrection of the Lord Jesus. And God's grace*

was so powerfully at work in them all that there were no needy persons among them." —Acts 4:32-34

Result:

"How pleasant it is when brothers dwell together in unity! For there the Lord bestows his blessing, even life forevermore." — Psalm 133:1, 3

Result:

"...Be one as we (Jesus and the Father) are one. I in them and you in me. May they be brought to complete unity to let the world know that you have sent me and have loved them even as you have loved me." —John 17:22-23 (Jesus' prayer for His followers)

Result:

Disunity breaks God's heart because it stops the flow of blessing, drains His people of power, and prevents the lost from seeing the true heart of a loving God. If we honor God by walking in unity, we will fulfill His call on our lives to support others to answer their call.

ASK

Are you grateful for the many amenities of a personal relationship with Christ? Take a moment to "count your many blessings... name them one by one."

_____

_____

_____

_____

Consider the results of unity: power, blessing and a witness to the lost. In which area do you need the help of the Holy Spirit to live in greater effectiveness?

_____

_____

Has it ever occurred to you that one hundred pianos all tuned to the same fork are automatically tuned to each other? They are of one accord by being tuned, not to each other, but to another standard to which each one must individually bow. So one hundred worshippers meeting together, each one looking away to Christ, are in heart nearer to each other than they could possibly be were they to become "unity" conscious and turn their eyes away from God to strive for closer fellowship. Social religion is perfected when private religion is purified. —A.W. Tozer[9]

The VIP Treatment

PHILIPPIANS 2:3-4

TODAY'S VERSE

"Do nothing out of selfish ambition or vain conceit, but in humility consider others better than yourselves. Each of you should look not only to your own interests, but also to the interests of others."
—Philippians 2:3-4

At the 2017 Academy Awards, celebrities received gift bags that included over $100,000 in gifts and amenities. The lavish Oscar "Swag Bags" included patches that keep you from sweating and a stay at a luxurious villa on Kuai's South Shore. However, long before Hollywood defined luxury, Paul gave us the true meaning of the VIP Treatment.[10]

AMPLIFY

We are to treat others as a VIP (Very Important Person). Most VIP's are familiar with the red carpet, which serves as a symbol of fame and achievement. God wants us to roll out the red carpet for others through our attitude and actions. We love the way He asks us to when we see others as worthy of preferential treatment. **When we recognize all God has done for us, we reconcile to walk in unity.** Pride is behind the desire to see "self" advanced.

Look at the beginning of verse 3 above and state what Paul identifies as the enemy of unity and harmony in the church:

LIVING BY THE SPIRIT

We can't be simultaneously led by the Spirit and driven by selfish ambition. Look up Galatians 5:16-26. I have included verses 16-18 below.

> *"So I say, live by the Spirit, and you will not gratify the desires of the sinful nature. For the sinful nature desires what is contrary to the Spirit and the Spirit what is contrary to the sinful nature. They are in conflict with each other, so that you do not do what you want. But if you are led by the Spirit, you are not under law."*

List some of the acts of our sin nature given in verses 19-21:

_____

_____

What do these verses tell us about those who live by the sin nature? They will not:

_____

_____

List the fruit of the Spirit given in verses 22-26:

_____

_____

This passage clearly shows us that our sin nature is in direct conflict with what the Spirit desires to develop in us. We must crucify our flesh if we want to keep in step with the Spirit.

APPLY

In January 2011, I joined a team of forty-four people working with Worldserve International to put clean water wells in Maasai villages. Our mission required traveling to Tanzania to climb Mount Kilimanjaro, Africa's tallest mountain. The six-day climb took our team through four ecosystems and breathtaking terrain.

The mountain, standing at 19,340 feet, proved to be a challenge for all of us. Each day involved a full day of climbing. The fourth day offered the ominous but rewarding experience of climbing the Barranco Wall. This was a key day for me. I was severely nauseated and having a tough time focusing during the afternoon hike.

As we hiked through Karanga Valley, I was running on empty and getting lower each hour. I had just enough phone battery to listen to worship music as inspiration. I still treasure those hours with God. He ministered to me and literally led me through the valley. I remember looking up and thinking, *"I'm so done. There's no way I can get up this."* I leaned forward and put my head on my poles. I dumped the water from my backpack to lighten my load and increase my chances of making it. I struggled to breathe. At my lowest point, a guide gently stepped in front of me said, *"Just follow my pace. Follow my steps."* When I looked up, I felt so overwhelmed, but I slowly put one foot in front of the other. I kept my head down and followed his feet. He led me to Barafu Camp, Base Camp of the Summit at 15,260 feet.

God used this vivid spiritual analogy of following His footsteps and listening only to His voice in tough times. I thought of Galatians 5:25, "Now that we live by the Spirit, let us keep in step with the Spirit." Follow His pace, His lead. I knew during these hours that I would not submit. I cried and breathed in the presence of God. I had my own personal summit at sundown on the edge of the cliff at Barafu Camp.

When we keep in step with the Spirit rather than live by our flesh, we look to the interests of others. This is what the guide did for me on the mountain. He could have focused on his own discomfort, but he chose to help me deal with mine. His compassion and companionship inspired me. Keeping in step with the Spirit means choosing to walk in unity. This allows God to release favor into your life and the lives of others.

THE VIP WARDROBE

Well, girls, as we all know, every VIP needs a wardrobe. Colossians 3:12-14 tells us what it is.

"Therefore, as God's chosen people, holy and dearly loved, clothe yourselves with compassion, kindness, humility, gentleness and patience. Bear with each other and forgive one another if any of you has a grievance against someone. Forgive as the Lord forgave you. And over all these virtues put on love, which binds them all together in perfect unity."

Are you wearing the wardrobe God has custom designed for you?

_____

_____

Which piece is missing from your closet?

_____

_____

Allow God to take you through the necessary process to become the woman He is calling you to be. As we embrace the dynamic duo of humility and unity, we will experience God's blessing and power.

ASK

Is it possible your motive for serving is driven by selfish ambition?

_____

_____

Would those who know you best say you live an others-minded life? If not, how can you roll out the red carpet for someone this week?

_____

_____

People are often unreasonable and self-centered. Forgive them anyway.
If you are kind, people may accuse you of ulterior motives. Be kind anyway.
If you are honest, people may cheat you. Be honest anyway.
If you find happiness, people may be jealous. Be happy anyway.
The good you do today may be forgotten tomorrow. Do good anyway.
Give the world the best you have and it may never be enough. Give your best anyway.
For you see, in the end, it is between you and God. It was never between you and them anyway. —Mother Teresa[11]

PHILIPPIANS 2:3-4

A Picture of Humility

PHILIPPIANS 2:3-4

TODAY'S VERSE

> *"Do nothing out of selfish ambition or vain conceit but in humility consider others better than yourselves. Each of you should look not only to your own interests but also to the interests of others."*
> —Philippians 2:3-4

Today's verses give us the key to developing and maintaining unity: humility. Our study is brief as we will take the next two days to consider the picture of humility through our ultimate example, Jesus Christ.

AMPLIFY

HUMILITY

Humility is the posture of a yielded heart. Look up the definition of humility and write down some key phrases.

Now write the definition of humility in your own words.

_____

_____

APPLY

We grow in unity when we walk in humility. Let's look at humility in action.

- **A Renewed Mind:** Romans 12:10 tells us to honor one another above yourselves. Only a mind renewed by the Holy Spirit could do this!
- **A Guarded Tongue:** Galatians 5:13-14 says, "You, my brothers, were called to be free. But do not use your freedom to indulge the sinful nature; rather, serve one another in love. The entire law is summed up in a single command: 'Love your neighbor as yourself'. If you keep on biting and devouring each other, watch out or you will be destroyed by each other."
- **A Submitted Spirit:** Ephesians 5:21 instructs us to submit to one another out of reverence for Christ.

ASK

Take a couple minutes for a Humility Inventory:

Does your thought life reveal a renewed mind?

_____

_____

Do you guard your tongue or do you have a habit of "biting and devouring" others?

_____

_____

Is your spirit submitted to the Lord, or do you fight for your own way?

_____

_____

We yield to the Holy Spirit by asking Him to reveal areas in these three places where He needs to have complete ownership. I'm in this with you, friend.

Prayer Challenge: *Help me to walk in true humility to see others through Your eyes, to honor others, and to submit to others out of reverence for You. Let my focus be to please You and further*

Your kingdom. Help me to be filled with the Spirit to the extent that the fruit evident in my life shows genuine concern for others. I want to be able to submit to You and others because of the Holy Spirit giving me a renewed mind and guarded tongue. Help me to remember that in unity there is freedom for You to operate in power. Amen.

SESSION 4 / DAY 4

A Servant's Attitude

PHILIPPIANS 2:5-8

TODAY'S VERSE

"Your attitude should be the same as that of Christ Jesus, who, being in very nature God, did not consider equality with God something to be grasped, but made himself nothing, taking the very nature of a servant, being made in human likeness. And being found in appearance as a man, he humbled himself and became obedient to death—even death on a cross."

—Philippians 2:5-8

Our attitude reflects our thought processes, beliefs, and behaviors. Contrary to our culture, Christ's attitude is one of self-sacrificial love and servanthood. We are called to emulate His radically different demeanor. He demonstrated complete submission through the degrading and cruel death on a cross. He died as someone cursed, taking upon Himself the sins of the world. He ransomed humanity out of obedience to the will of His Father, purchasing our salvation and eternal life.

AMPLIFY

Please read today's verses several times, slowly, and perhaps aloud. We have a greater appreciation for Christ's example when we look at key phrases in today's passage.

IN VERY NATURE GOD

In Philippians 2:6, "being in very nature God," means *to have the essential form of God.*

Romans 9:5, among other Scriptures, tells us that Jesus is fully God. This is a key Scriptural truth that separates Christianity from all other world religions or cults. Jesus Christ is co-equal with God the Father. This is the status and privilege that inevitably follows from being "in nature" God.

SOMETHING TO BE GRASPED

Christ did not consider that exalted position something He could not give up. Jesus took the full reality of a servant, making it His identity.

What does this tell us about the way we view our rights?

_____

_____

MADE HIMSELF NOTHING

This literally means He emptied Himself, not by giving up his Deity, but by laying aside His glory.

APPLY

LEADING THROUGH SERVING

We find one of the most poignant illustrations of Jesus as a servant in John 13. Please turn to this passage and read the powerful story of Jesus washing His disciples' feet. Jesus shows us that no servant is greater than his master, nor is a messenger greater than the one who sent him. Foot washing was a menial task, and no one else volunteered to do this. Jesus even washed the feet of Judas, knowing that Judas would imminently betray Him. Jesus' selfless service challenges us to step up. After you have read it, look at the key phrases I have pulled out for you and consider how they apply to our lives. Then, add what each phrase means to you.

"Jesus knew that the hour had come for him to leave this world and go to the father." —John 13:1

What this meant for Jesus: Jesus found His identity and purpose in the Father. All things were under His control.

How this applies to us: We find our destiny in the Father.

What this means to me:

_____

_____

"Having loved His own who were in the world, He loved them to the end." —John 13:1

What this meant for Jesus: Jesus obeyed by serving. He demonstrated the full extent of His love in tangible ways.

How this applies to us: We show others we love them by serving them.

What this means to me:

_____

_____

"Jesus knew that the Father had put all things under His power…" —John 13:3

What this meant for Jesus: The Father was in control.

How this applies to us: We should release control and do whatever God asks us to do.

What this means to me:

_____

_____

"He got up from the meal…" —John 13:4

What this meant for Jesus: He got up from the position of being served to take the position of serving.

How this applies to us: Our focus must be on meeting the needs of others.

What this means to me:

_____

_____

"...Took off his outer clothing..." —John 13:4

What this meant for Jesus: He wanted His disciples to see His example of true humility.

How this applies to us: We must be willing to take off external things and make ourselves vulnerable to others.

What this means to me:

_____

_____

"'No,' said Peter, 'you shall never wash my feet.'" —John 13:8

What this meant for Jesus: Peter resisted Jesus because he did not agree with or understand what Jesus was doing. Jesus did not let anything deter Him from doing the Father's will.

How this applies to us: We must learn to surrender our will and allow God to define the "what and how" we live our lives. His ways are higher and better than ours.

What this means to me:

_____

_____

John ends this chapter by telling us, "Now that you know these things you will be blessed by doing them." **If you want to live in God's blessings, you can't shortcut God's process.** The journey of finding joy when life is out of focus travels through the terrain of servanthood. When we trust our Heavenly Father is in control of all things, we rest in His character even when we don't understand our circumstances.

ASK

We've studied how Jesus served others by washing their feet. What is one practical way you can serve those closest to you? Put that into action this week.

_____

_____

Prayer Challenge: *Thank you for making Yourself nothing that I might have forgiveness of sins and eternal life. Create in me a new heart and a willing spirit, surrendered and yielded to You. Teach me to walk in Your ways, following Your example of a servant. Renew my thoughts, beliefs, motives, and give me a new attitude. Amen.*

A New Song

PHILIPPIANS 2:9-11

TODAY'S VERSE

"Therefore God exalted him to the highest place and gave him the name that is above every name, that at the name of Jesus every knee should bow, in heaven and on earth and under the earth, and every tongue confess that Jesus Christ is Lord, to the glory of God the Father." —Philippians 2:9-11

Jesus is the antithesis of the selfish ambition Paul warned us of in Philippians 1. Today, we'll see the results of His obedience.

AMPLIFY

EXALTED TO THE HIGHEST PLACE

What does it mean for God to exalt Jesus to the highest place? Hebrews 1:2-3 gives us insight.

"But in these last days he has spoken to us by his Son, whom he appointed heir of all things, and through whom also he made the universe. The Son is the radiance of God's glory and the exact representation of his being, sustaining all things by his powerful word. After he had provided purification for sins, he sat down at the right hand of the Majesty in heaven."

List the statements this passage makes about Jesus:

_____

_____

_____

_____

Jesus is the heir, the inheritor of God's estate. He is seated, indicating that the priestly work was finished. In the Old Testament, the Jewish Rabbis fulfilled the duties of a priest, continually making sacrifices for the atonement of the nation's sins. They were forbidden to sit in the temple because this work was never completed. When Jesus became the sacrifice, He completed the work of atoning for sins and sat down at the right hand of the Father. He was given the name (title, rank, or position) "Jesus," "Kurios" in Greek, meaning Lord.[12]

God's design is that all people everywhere should worship and serve Jesus as Lord. One day, every knee shall bow and every tongue confess that Jesus is Lord. We worship Jesus because His obedience to the cross bought our freedom. He reigns victorious over sin and the grave. Revelation 5 peels back the curtain to reveal all of heaven worshipping the risen Savior. The harmonies of Jesus as obedient Son blend with Jesus as overcoming King...and heaven sings a new song.

"The four living creatures and the twenty-four elders fell down before the Lamb. Each one had a harp and they were holding golden bowls full of incense, which are the prayers of God's people. And they sang a new song, saying:

"You are worthy to take the scroll and to open its seals, because you were slain, and with your blood you purchased for God persons from every tribe and language and people and nation.

You have made them to be a kingdom and priests to serve our God, and they will reign on the earth." Then I looked and heard the voice of many angels, numbering thousands upon thousands, and ten thousand times ten thousand. They encircled the throne and the living creatures and the elders. In a loud voice they were saying:

"Worthy is the Lamb, who was slain, to receive power and wealth and wisdom and strength and honor and glory and praise!"

Then I heard every creature in heaven and on earth and under the earth and on the sea, and all that is in them, saying:

"To him who sits on the throne and to the Lamb be praise and honor and glory and power, for ever and ever!"

The four living creatures said, "Amen," and the elders fell down and worshiped."

APPLY

Your obedience is your worship. **God takes the sounds we struggle to surrender and composes a beautiful melody from a submitted heart.** We offer Him brokenness and He writes hope. You don't have to live shackled by sin or paralyzed by pain. It's time for you to sing a new song... the song God is writing over your life. His heavenly harmonies are crafted from our tender places, made sacred through surrender.

We are created with a God-given thirst for joy. When we view our circumstances and relationships through the lens of His perspective, we see His purpose—even when we don't understand. As we walk in tandem with unity and humility, we discover the joy in harmony. Girls, let's stop playing the dissonant chord of pride and listen for the song of joy. Heaven is writing your song.

ASK

What impacted you the most from this week's lesson?

_____

_____

"WOMAN IN LOVE" / Music and Lyrics by Angela Donadio
From "This Journey"

Not the same girl I used to be
Feels kinda strange to be this free
Give me a minute and I'll tell you what He means to me.

He gave me an invitation
In spite of all my reservations
To come and sit at His table

And write His name on my heart;
Now I'm lavished for a lifetime
Gifts like flowers in the springtime,
And waking new every morning
With mercies again;

I'm just a woman in love,
With her Maker,
A woman in love,
Couldn't take me away if you tried
There's nowhere that I'd rather be than with Him,
I'm just a woman in love.

I'm amazed that He can recognize
This fragile heart behind each new disguise,
And find a way to remind me
How much my hands have to hold;
And if all of this is not enough
(I wear) garments of grace that I'm not worthy of
So far beyond my expectation
More than redeemer, my friend.

(Chorus)
Please forgive me if I don't apologize
For this feeling I am struggling to describe.
I only know that I am not afraid to show
That I'm in love.

Not the same girl I used to be
Feels kinda strange to be this free
Give me a lifetime and I'll tell You what He means to me.

"This Journey" Available on www.angeladonadio.com and iTunes

—— *Session 5* ——

Sacrifice and Service

JOY IN OBEDIENCE –
PHILIPPIANS CHAPTER 2

DAY 1 / OBEYING ON PURPOSE—CH 2:12-13

DAY 2 / SHINE LIKE STARS—CH 2:14-16

DAY 3 / SHINE LIKE STARS (PART 2)—CH 2:14-16

DAY 4 / POURED OUT—CH 2:17-18

DAY 5 / A SUPPORT SYSTEM—CH 2:19-30

Obeying on Purpose

PHILIPPIANS 2:12-13

TODAY'S VERSE

"Therefore, my dear friends, as you have always obeyed—not only in my presence but now much more in my absence—continue to work out your salvation with fear and trembling, for it is God who works in you to will and to act according to His good purpose."
—Philippians 2:12-13

In 2015, I met Kenyan athletes training for the Summer Olympics in Eldoret, Kenya. I witnessed the focus, dedication, and perseverance of these runners. They train for years, demonstrating tremendous commitment, to win a single race—some lasting barely a minute. It's ludicrous to imagine an Olympic athlete running aimlessly all over the track with no sense of purpose. They run to win.

1 Corinthians 9:24 states, "Do you not know that in a race all the runners run but only one gets the prize? Run in such a way as to get the prize." In today's verse, Paul instructs us to work out our salvation, running the race of life with resolve and determination. Girlfriends, our Christian walk is not about earning our salvation through works. However, we are not to become lazy and lackadaisical about our relationship with Christ. Rather, we commit to the Holy Spirit's process in our life, allowing Him to mature us through sacrifice and service.

AMPLIFY

What is the first word of today's verse?

_____

When you see a "therefore", you need to know what it is there for. "Therefore" lets us know that today's passage is a continuation of Philippians 2:9-11, which shares Jesus' reward for His obedience. We are encouraged to follow His example in our quest for joy.

OBEY ON PURPOSE

God calls us to obedience and holiness, so we can grow and produce fruit. Some of us may flinch at the word obedience, but keep in mind that God always blesses obedience. We reap the fruit of the Spirit when we are intentional about obeying.

2 Peter 1:5-8 contains a recipe for godly living. List the ingredients necessary to mature in Christ and produce fruit.

_____

_____

_____

_____

FEAR AND TREMBLING

When we fear God, we treat Him with reverence. Exodus 14:31 narrates how the Israelites "feared the Lord and put their trust in Him" when they saw how He handled the Egyptians. The knowledge of the power of the Lord humbled the Israelites. Likewise, we learn to work out our salvation with fear and trembling by trusting God's character and obeying His voice.

APPLY

When we fear the Lord, we won't hold onto things that are not pleasing to Him. We find joy when life is out of focus by staying sensitive to the Spirit. Difficult circumstances tempt us to become hard-hearted and cold. Obedience means we are willing to release unmet expectations and fix our eyes on Jesus. Unresolved disappointments turn into bitterness and resentment.

Resentment is quicksand. When you hold onto disappointment, you can easily become stuck, robbing you of joy. Nothing is worth missing God's best. If you're in the quagmire of resentment, take a moment to give every unmet expectation to the Lord. Ask Him to soften your heart and renew your trust in Him. When we choose obedience we find joy.

Review today's passage, Philippians 2:12-13.

Who works in us?

_____

_____

He is working "to will and to act according to" what?

_____

_____

Stop and think about that for a moment. God is at work in you, through you and for you. You don't have to do this alone. God meets our obedience and human effort with divine help. Joy-thirsty women, you are valuable to God. Your life matters. God is working in you to act according to His great purposes for you.

ASK

Reread the recipe for godly living found 2 Peter 1:5-8. Are you missing any ingredients, slowing down your quest for joy? If so, confess that to the Lord and ask for His help.

_____

_____

Shine Like Stars

PHILIPPIANS 2:14-16

TODAY'S VERSE

"Do everything without complaining or arguing so that you may become pure and blameless children of God without fault in a crooked and depraved generation in which you shine like stars in the universe as you hold out the word of life."

—Philippians 2:14-16

———————————————————————

Some of my fondest childhood memories include visits to a planetarium. I remember leaning back in my seat and listening to the soothing atmospheric sounds, spellbound by stars. It's no surprise that my favorite ride at Disney World is Space Mountain. The ride is fabulous, but what I love most are the countless stars giving you the sensation of riding through space.

On a clear night, you'll most likely find me outside gazing at the starry sky.

Today's verse compares our lives to stars in the universe. A star contains the same DNA as the sun. It is a "mini-sun," a light in the darkness of the night sky. When stars twinkle, they shine with rapidly intermittent gleams, or shimmering. We contain the same DNA as Jesus Christ, created in the image of God. Let's look deeper into this concept, to discover how we shine like stars.[13]

AMPLIFY

Philippians 2:14 contains six of the most challenging words in this book, if not the entire New Testament.

Write the first six words of today's passage:

_____

_____

We complain when we're discontent with the will of God. An argumentative spirit is an outward expression of an inward lack of trust in God. If we want to radiate joy, we must pull up roots of discontent.

SHINING FOR GOD

When we shine with the light of Christ, we contrast the darkness around us. To "shine" means *to reflect light, be bright or to glow*. It also means *to polish, be visible, be brilliant, and excel*. Perhaps you're uncomfortable with the idea of standing out. But God has created us in His image to be light-bearers in a murky world.

THE WORD OF LIFE

Review today's verses. Paul states that we shine like stars as we hold out what?

_____

_____

We shine when we keep our grip on the Word of God as our life manual. When we view situations through the lens of His Word, the love of Christ is visible in our actions.

THE LIGHT OF THE WORLD

Several Scriptures use the words "reflect" and "light" when describing what it means to shine.

Read the account of Paul's conversion in Acts 9:1-19.

What happened in Verse 3?

_____

_____

What does Verse 8-9 tell us was the result of the light?

_____

_____

What happens when Ananias lays his hands on Paul in Verses 17-19?

_____

_____

Light played a significant role in one of Paul's most defining moments. When he met Jesus, the light of the world, he was forever changed. This divine encounter left Paul temporarily blind. God removed the scales from Paul's eyes just as He removes things that hinder us from having clear spiritual vision. Grumbling and complaining blurs our lens on life, keeping us from loving the life we see. Our thoughts are transformed when we come face to face with Jesus.

We can continually enter His presence where He illuminates us with the light of His love. We shine as we reflect the glory of God, which only comes by being with Him. You were created to display the glory of God.

APPLY

MIRROR IMAGE

As we connect with God, we increase our ability to shine for Him. 2 Corinthians 3:14-18 gives us more insight into what takes place. What does Verse 18 say about us?

_____

_____

God continually transforms us into His likeness, becoming more and more like Him. We reflect His glory like a mirror reflects an image. We may not like what a mirror shows, a few new wrinkles, or puffy eyes from lack of sleep, but it doesn't lie. The mirror of God's Word is perfect, and as we look into it, we become like the image of Christ.

Think about a glow in the dark toy. What do you have to do to it for it to glow?

_____

_____

Glow in the dark toys must be charged by the light before their luminous properties show forth in the dark. Light is necessary to make God's creative works visible and public. We cannot spend time with Him without exposure to the light of who He is. **When we're charged by God's character, we're content with His will.**

Look again at today's passage. Philippians 2:15 identifies characteristics of a life marked by contentment. What are they?

_____

_____

ASK

Hold the mirror of God's Word up to your heart. Do you see any discontent with the will of God? I challenge you this week to keep a written record of every time you find yourself complaining or arguing. Ask God to transform your mind to see His perspective.

_____

_____

Are you comfortable standing out for God? Why or why not?

_____

_____

Prayer Challenge: *Lord, help me to do everything without complaining or arguing. I repent of any discontent in my heart. Help me to reflect Your love and character as I spend time in Your presence. Let that be my top priority.*

Shine Like Stars (Part 2)

PHILIPPIANS 2:14-16

TODAY'S VERSE

"Do everything without complaining or arguing so that you may become pure and blameless children of God without fault in a crooked and depraved generation in which you shine like stars in the universe as you hold out the word of life."

—Philippians 2:14-16

AMPLIFY

LIGHT IS ARMOR

God wants us to shine so His light will permeate the darkness. His character in us breathes fresh air into a polluted society. Romans 13:12 provides a unique perspective on light: "Let us put aside the deeds of darkness and put on the armor of light."

In the same way armor protects a warrior, godly living protects our hearts. If we are reflecting God's light, it should show in our choices. Choices determine our actions and shape our character, often formed in the fire of adversity. Previously, we studied the full armor of God. Try to list the pieces of armor by memory. If you need help, turn to Ephesians 6.

(Hint—We find one commonly overlooked item in Verse 18!)

_____

_____

_____

_____

When facing attacks from the enemy, we must fight in God's strength, not our own. When we are dressed in the armor of light, we shine from the inside out. Ephesians 5:8-14 says, "For you were once darkness but you are light in the Lord. Have nothing to do with the fruitless deeds of darkness, but rather expose them. Everything exposed by the light becomes visible for it is light that makes everything visible."

In God's mercy, He will bring to light things in our lives that need attention. The Holy Spirit convicts us and corrects us for our good and His glory. **God exposes sin not to shame us, but to heal us.** An unrepentant spirit keeps us from experiencing joy. But God, the Master Surgeon, cuts away dead things to bring us to life. He calls us out of the shadows and into the fullness of His light.

APPLY

The enemy wants us to believe we are safer when we hide our light. He knows that when we cower in fear, we become powerless and ineffective. But when we believe God created us with purpose, we look for tangible ways to impact others. Think about the following sources of light and describe their purpose. I will get you started.

Fire—Brings warmth, critical for survival (food, boiling water), hard to contain

Desk Lamp—_____

Flashlight— _____

Sunlight— _____

Stars— _____

Light is not passive. It invades, permeates, and drives out darkness. This is part of our purpose; but first, we must allow God to push out the darkness in us before we can be a light to others. The Holy Spirit illuminates our hearts and minds to respond to His call with obedience.

What does Matthew 5:14-16 tell us about our purpose?

_____

_____

Why should we let our lives shine before men?

_____

_____

Dear friend, your obedience brings glory to your Heavenly Father. He gives us the desire and the strength to obey His word. As we wear the armor of light, He shines on us so we can shine for Him.

ASK

One of the definitions of shine is to polish. What is one area that you need to allow God to polish so that you can shine for Him?

_____

_____

"This little light of mine, I'm gonna let it shine. Hide it under a bushel, no! I'm gonna let it shine." What are your "bushels," the safe places and times in which you hide your light from others?

_____

_____

Prayer Challenge: _Lord, whatever it takes, I desire to serve You with my whole heart. Work in me, removing all fears so I can truly shine for You. Thank You for giving me the armor of light to protect me and guard me. You are the lamp for my feet and the light on my path._

Poured Out

PHILIPPIANS 2:17-18

TODAY'S VERSE

"But even if I am being poured out like a drink offering on the sacrifice and service coming from your faith, I am glad and rejoice with all of you. So you too should be glad and rejoice with me." —Philippians 2:17-18

Paul found joy in obedience, even when he didn't know what lay ahead. His entire ministry was marked by sacrifice and service. With the impending possibility of death, Paul chose to rejoice, making his life a thanksgiving offering to God.

AMPLIFY

BUT...EVEN IF...NO MATTER WHAT...

"But" is a small word with big implications. Although Paul can't see around the next corner, his faith is firmly grounded in God and not dependent on an earthly outcome. Paul is clearly telling his readers that even if the worst happens, he will rejoice because of their faith. He understood the role he played in God's plan and in the lives of others.

Write today's verses in your own handwriting and share what stands out to you the most and why.

_____

_____

_____

From what you just wrote, how would you define Paul's role? (What does Paul say that he is?)

_____

_____

Why does he rejoice?

_____

_____

POURED OUT AS A DRINK OFFERING

We need to read Genesis 28:10-22 to understand the context of Paul's statement in Philippians 2:17.

What does Jacob do with the stone he had just slept on the night before?

_____

_____

Jacob identified the stone as a place of sacrifice and an altar of worship. He used oil to consecrate it and make it holy. When something is consecrated, it is set apart for God's use and glory. In today's verse from Philippians, Paul is identifying with a priest, describing himself as a "drink offering" being poured over the people that he loved.

Exodus 29 gives us context and helps us understand what this really means. As God gives Moses instructions for the consecration of the priests, He tells Aaron and his sons, who act as priests over the Israelites, to make a sacrifice on the altar.

List the items in the sacrifice from Exodus 29:

Two one-year-old _____

Two quarts (a tenth of an ephah) of _____

One quart (a quarter of a hin) of _____

One quart (a quarter of a hin) of _____

God chose the specific elements of the offerings. The priests in the Old Testament made these sacrifices to atone for the sins of the people. As an expression of making restitution for sin, the priest would offer a burnt offering and pour out oil or wine as a drink offering. Oil is extracted through a time-consuming process of handpicking olives, removing impurities, and crushing the olive.

The list in Exodus 29 was a representation of Jesus' sacrifice that would come many years later. Jesus is our Passover Lamb, the Lamb who takes away the sins of the world. Just as manna fed the Israelites, Jesus is the Bread of Life. Jesus agonized and surrendered His will in the Garden of Gethsemane on the Mount of Olives, anticipating the crushing that was to come. The blood of Jesus was poured out for our salvation. We no longer need to make sacrifices for our sins because Jesus paid our debt in full at Calvary.

APPLY

Romans 12:1-2 is one of my life verses: "In view of God's mercy, present your bodies as living sacrifices, holy and pleasing to God which is your spiritual act of worship."

What does this verse tell us is our offering today?

_____

_____

We present our lives as an offering in view of (or because of) what?

_____

_____

Romans 6:13 gives us additional insight about offering our bodies as a sacrifice. "Do not offer your body to sin; offer yourselves to God as those who have been brought from death to life, instruments of righteousness. Be what you already are—dead to sin, alive to God. Do not let sin reign in you." As we make our lives an offering to the Lord, we experience true freedom. When we find freedom, we find joy.

Paul could live in joy because of the impact his life was having on the church in Philippi. He rejoiced in their faith, regardless of the cost to him personally. He offered his life as a sacrifice through service and asked them to rejoice with him—despite what they saw him going through.

Although Paul's life was not a literal drink offering, he allowed himself to be "poured out" for the Gospel. Perhaps you are going through a season of crushing. Girlfriends, God extracts the precious oil of His anointing through our trials. We can find joy—even when life is out of focus—when we pour ourselves out in obedience.

ASK

Describe a place of crushing in your life. Perhaps the wound is fresh or perhaps a scar has formed where healing took place. In what ways do you see God extracting the oil of gladness out of mourning?

_____

_____

How does God's mercy serve as a motivator for us to offer our lives to Him?

_____

_____

A Support System

PHILIPPIANS 2:19-30

TODAY'S VERSE

"I hope in the Lord Jesus to send Timothy to you soon that I may also be cheered when I receive news about you. I have no one else like him who takes a genuine interest in your welfare. For everyone looks out for their own interests, not those of Jesus Christ. However, you know that Timothy has proved himself because as a son without his father, he has served with me in the work of the Gospel. I hope to send him as soon as I see how things go with me. I am confident in the Lord that I myself will come soon. However, I think it is necessary to send back to you Epaphroditus, my brother, fellow worker and fellow soldier, who is also your messenger, whom you sent to take care of my needs. For he longs for all of you and is distressed because you heard he was ill. Indeed, he almost died. But God had mercy on him, and not on him only but on me, to spare me sorrow upon sorrow. Therefore, I am all the more eager to send him so that when you see him again you may be glad and I may have less anxiety. Welcome him in the Lord with great joy, and honor men like him, because he almost died for the work of Christ, risking his life to make up for the help you could not give me." —Philippians 2:19-30

We are more than halfway through our study, "Finding Joy." When life blurs the lens of our perspective, we need women who help us see the truth of God's love clearly. You know who I mean. The experienced mom who speaks calm into the chaos of your life with two little ones. The resilient woman who weathered a painful season with a prodigal child when your son is breaking your heart. The compassionate wife who knows what it takes to hold on to a marriage when yours is crumbling. *Those* women...the support system who pray with us, cry with us, and hope with us.

Paul was no exception. He also needed good friends that he could depend on and trust in ministry. Philippians 2 introduces us to his most devoted support system, Timothy and Epaphroditus. Their importance to Paul shows us the value of strong relationships.

AMPLIFY

How does Paul describe Timothy?

_____

_____

TIMOTHY—PASSING THE BATON

Paul poured his life into Timothy, serving as a mentor for his "son in the faith." Paul writes an extended letter to him in first and second Timothy. Timothy had a Greek father, a Jewish Christian mom, and became a part of Paul's ministry after first meeting him in Lystra. On Paul's second visit, he saw something in Timothy that prompted him to extend an invitation to join his missionary journey. As a result, Timothy had an extensive ministry, accompanying Paul to Macedonia, Achaia, Corinth, Asia Minor and a long stretch in Ephesus. Paul trusted Timothy's knowledge of Scripture and ability to handle things without him. He left Timothy in Macedonia while he went to Ephesus, giving him specific commands to refute false doctrines.

1 Timothy 4 records the critical instructions provided to Timothy by Paul. Read this chapter and write them here. I have started the list for you.

- Don't let anyone look down on you because you're young.
- Don't neglect your gifts.
- _____
- _____
- _____

- _____
- _____

In Verse 12, Paul told Timothy to set an example in five areas. What are they?

_____

_____

In this passage, we see Paul, the spiritual giant of the New Testament, handing the baton to Timothy. Timothy has big shoes to fill. Paul is a legacy leader and is determined to ensure the work of the Gospel does not die with him.

How do you think Timothy felt? How would you feel following in the footsteps of Paul?

_____

_____

Have you ever been asked to fill big spiritual shoes? If so, describe that experience and how God equipped you for the challenge.

_____

_____

EPAPHRODITUS—RISKING IT ALL

Let's go back to today's verses, Philippians 2:19-30. What attributes does Paul write in his resume about Epaphroditus?

_____

_____

In looking at this list, it is obvious that Epaphroditus loved the church and the work of the ministry, even risking his own life for the Gospel and for Paul. Based on the lists you completed about Paul's partners in the faith, Timothy and Epaphroditus, why was Paul able to place such confidence in them?

_____

_____

Look again at Philippians 2:29: "Welcome him in the Lord with great joy and honor men like him because he almost died for the work of

Christ, risking his life to make up for the help you could not give me." The church of Philippi sent Epaphroditus to bring ministry resources to Paul. We don't know specific details, but he nearly died on the journey. According to this passage, how should we treat those who willingly place themselves in harm's way for the Gospel?

_____

_____

APPLY

Paul recognized the value of community, investing in the people he pastored and mentored. He dedicated his life to sacrifice and service, finding the joy in obedience. His sacrifice was rewarded with the advancement of the Gospel and the transformation of lives. Epaphroditus was a blessing to Paul and the church of Philippi, and the church was an important part of their ministry. Timothy encouraged Paul and Paul mentored Timothy. This outlines a critical spiritual principle: we are not created to live and minister in a vacuum.

Women, we need one another. **We are stronger when we support each other.** God is asking some of you to be a Paul, passing the baton to the next generation through your guidance. God is calling others of you to be a Timothy, filling big shoes and carry the Gospel through obedience. And yet others, He is breathing confidence into apprehensive places, inspiring you to follow Epaphroditus and risk it all for the kingdom.

Every day, we brush shoulders with other joy-thirsty women. As we connect through relationship, we provide a staunch support system that can brave the fierce winds of adversity. As you move forward this week in obedience, take the hand of the nervous woman next to you. You'll be one step closer to loving the life you see.

ASK

If you are a young or new believer, are you actively seeking out a mature mentor in Christ? If not, who could you talk to about supporting you in your Christian walk?

_____

_____

If you are mature in your Christian walk, are you mentoring another woman? If not, what is one step you could take today to reach out in support?

_____

_____

"POURED OUT" / Music and Lyrics by Angela Donadio
From "It's a New Day"

Show me how to walk by faith and not by sight
When I can't see past the darkness of this night
I will look up from this place, see the wonder of Your grace
And build an altar from the broken things in me,

Let my life be poured out as an offering to You
Let my life be poured out, I surrender to You,
Take my words, take my heart, take my life, every part,
Let it be poured out....

I believe that every word You say is true
So I choose to place all my hope in You
And in these times of desolation, I'll cry out in desperation
Be my shield and my tower, O God...

"It's A New Day" Available on www.angeladonadio.com and iTunes

Session 6

Temporary Pain, Eternal Gain

JOY IN TRANSFORMATION
PHILIPPIANS CHAPTER 3

DAY 1 / SAFEGUARD YOUR JOY—CH 3:1

DAY 2 / A NEW HEART—CH 3:3-4

DAY 3 / PAUL'S RÉSUMÉ ON FILE—CH 3:4-6

DAY 4 / THE GREAT REVERSAL—CH 3:7-9

DAY 5 / LIVING DEAD—CH 3:10-11

Safeguard Your Joy

PHILIPPIANS 3:1

TODAY'S VERSE

"Finally, my brothers, rejoice in the Lord! It is no trouble for you to write the same things to you again, and it is a safeguard for you."
—Philippians 3:1

Butterflies, originally called "flutterbys," are a striking portrait of transformation. I have come to love them for many reasons, and several rooms in my home display their splendor. I am intrigued by their unusual beauty and ability to pollenate and decorate our world. Their delicate wings dance in the wind and remind us of God's infinite creativity.

These little things have made a big impact on my life. First, there is the obvious parallel to my health crisis that resulted in a large scar running the length of my torso. A caterpillar, embracing the possibility of a new life as a butterfly, spins a cocoon. Her body completely dissolves and reforms. When the time is right, the cocoon splits down the middle. Tiny wings press into the open air and a lovely, entirely new creature emerges. I can relate to each step of this amazing, God-ordained process.

Secondly, there is my quite extensive list of butterfly sightings that I view as "God's fingerprints." I have encountered butterflies on countless occasions, particularly on trips to Africa. For example, while on a trip to West Africa, I needed hospitalization for a violent allergic reaction to something I ate. Before the doctor could treat me, I needed to pay for the electricity in my small, bare hospital room. I spent the night in the most primitive of surroundings, but slept on sheets covered with—*yep, you guessed it*—butterflies. One of my lowest and loneliest moments occurred in East Africa. After a long day of riding on unpaved roads, I desperately needed a shower. Carsick and homesick by evening, I struggled as much with my attitude as with the cold, trickling water. After a feeble attempt, I reached for a towel. Embroidered on this thin, scratchy hotel towel, was—*yep, you guessed it*—a butterfly.

While ministering in Tanzania, I enjoyed a brief respite in between our hectic ministry schedule in Ruaha National Game Park. My companion had returned home due to the death of a family member. I spent two breathtaking days on safari and two lonely and challenging nights sleeping by myself in a large banda tent, surrounded by nature and wild animals. Although this is one of my favorite places on earth, being alone on a game reserve at night with no electricity or cell service is frightening. I tried my best to get a few hours of sleep while being serenaded by lions and elephants outside my tent. To add insult to injury, I ate something at dinner the second night that prompted the same reaction in my body as whatever had landed me in the hospital years earlier. I spent a tough night making numerous trips to the bathroom, unzipping my tent, watching for animals, and longing for home. The next morning, while the team went on the last game drive, I stayed back to rest. They moved me to a banda closer to the main camp where I lay in a hammock and slept. Embellishing the hammock cloth was—*yep, you guessed it*—butterflies.

My journals are full of stories about butterflies God has sent my way, reminding me of God's love. Transformation is not an effortless process, whether for a butterfly, or for us. We must push through the difficulties we encounter to become all God wants us to be. Keep in mind, joy-thirsty women, that our temporary pain leads to eternal gain.

AMPLIFY

SAFEGUARD YOUR JOY

This study came to life after the Lord warned me to guard my joy. The pain of adversity affects our temperament and personal interactions, prompting Paul to remind the Philippians to rejoice. Without apology, he stresses the importance of rejoicing in and under all circumstances. My prayer is that you will learn to safeguard your joy and experience God's fullness in your life.

APPLY

In 1 Samuel Chapter 1, we meet Hannah, a woman who experienced the joy of transformation. Take a moment to read her heart-wrenching story. She desperately wanted a child. In the ancient world, a woman's worth was determined by the number of male children she bore. Motherhood was the aim of all married women, and life was hard for a childless woman. Blamed for her barrenness, her husband often divorced her or added another wife to the household.

Married to Elkanah, Hannah's life was made difficult by the taunts of Peninnah, her husband's other wife. Even though the Bible tells us that he loved Hannah most, Peninnah made fun of her because she had no children, making life almost unbearable.

What does 1 Samuel 1:10-11 tell us Hannah was praying for while at the great religious festival?

_____

_____

What does Hannah offer to do?

_____

_____

In answer to Hannah's prayer, Samuel, the prophet-priest of Israel was born. Perhaps Hannah wrestled with the temptation to break her promise once she held Samuel in her arms. To give birth to a child and bond with him for several years before giving him to someone else must have been agonizing. However, Hannah was a woman of her word. She weaned Samuel between three and five years of age and delivered him to the House of the Lord at Shiloh to begin his service to God under the care of Eli, the priest.

Read 1 Samuel 2:1-10 to hear Hannah's poignant prayer after she gave Samuel to the Lord.

Write the words to 1 Samuel 2:1 below.

_____

_____

From the time that Hannah gave Samuel to be raised by Eli, she made a yearly visit to see her son. What do verses 18-21 tell us Hannah brought with her?

_____

_____

With every thread, she gently wove in her tears and prayers for Samuel. She loved her son, but she gave him over to the God who gave him to her. Her temporary pain in selflessly giving Samuel to the Lord resulted in eternal gain. She rejoiced in her transformation from bitterness and barrenness to joy and fullness. God rewarded Hannah with more children and a first-born son that faithfully served God his entire life, becoming one of the most beloved rulers in Israel.

As women, we can identify with Hannah in one of two ways. Which of the following statements do you most identify with and why?

1. God has transformed a situation in my life. (If so, describe that experience here.)

_____

_____

2. I need God to transform a situation in my life. (If so, describe that desire here.)

_____

_____

STANDING AT SHILOH

In 2015, I had the privilege of traveling to the Holy Land with Lysa TerKeurst, president of Proverbs 31 Ministries. In addition to the locations normally visited on a trip to Israel, our group received the offer to choose one optional site. I jumped at the chance to visit Shiloh, even though it meant traveling by bullet-proof bus through a volatile region. After hundreds of years in a portable tabernacle, Shiloh is the site of the first permanent tabernacle, where Israel worshiped for over three centuries. The dusty ruins, undergoing archeological excavation, are the exact place where Hannah came thousands of years ago to beseech God for a son. My breath caught in the back of my throat as I thought of the tears that wet the hallowed ground where I now stood.

I reflected silently on the countless times God listened to the desperate cries of my heart. I paused to thank Him for His faithfulness during seasons when adversity obscured His face. I whispered a prayer of gratitude for a God who would not only choose to reveal Himself through an earthly tabernacle but would make His home in me. The God that changed Hannah's life is the God that transforms us. He hears our cries and washes away our weariness. Time in His presence is a safeguard for our joy. You don't have to journey to Shiloh to experience His presence. **Your heart is the tabernacle that holds the treasure of His grace.**

Wherever you find yourself right this moment can become your personal Shiloh. I pray you receive a fresh revelation of His promise over your life as you place your trust in an unfailing God. The place of petition becomes holy ground when we allow Him to take our temporary pain and transform it for eternal gain.

ASK

Hannah safeguarded her joy by focusing on God's faithfulness. Reflect on God's faithfulness in your life. Why do you have a reason to rejoice today?

_____

_____

A New Heart

PHILIPPIANS 3:2-4

TODAY'S VERSE

"Watch out for those dogs, those men who do evil, those mutilators of the flesh. For it is we who are the circumcision, we who worship by the Spirit of God, who glory in Christ Jesus, who put no confidence in the flesh—though I have reasons for such confidence."
—Philippians 3:2-4

I must confess that when I first read today's verses, I was slightly intimidated by the subject matter. However, as I studied it, I became encouraged by the principles in God's Word. I'm praying they will bless you today, too.

AMPLIFY

FREEDOM IN CHRIST

Paul warned against the teaching of Jewish Christians who believed that some of the Old Testament practices established under the Law were still binding. These teachers, Judaizers, argued that Paul was not an authentic apostle. They accused him of trying to make the Gospel more appealing to the Gentiles by removing Jewish customs, including the practice of circumcision. They taught bondage to the Law, perverting the concept of grace. In Galatians 5, Paul writes a clear exposition about the freedom we have in Christ as opposed to salvation by works. We are justified by faith in Christ Jesus and sanctified (made holy) not through our works, but through the working of the Holy Spirit in us.

Turn to Galatians 5 to read the instructions Paul gave regarding false teaching about circumcision.

Write Galatians 5:4 in the space below.

_____

_____

What does this verse mean to you?

_____

_____

What does Paul tell us in Galatians 5:6?

_____

_____

AMPLIFY

Let's look at some key phrases in today's passage that help us to understand Paul's concerns.

DOGS, MEN WHO DO EVIL

Paul uses strong language to describe those who are teaching serious error, the same type of Jewish Christians he addressed in Galatians Chapter 5. Paul wants the new converts to understand they are saved by grace, not through fulfillment of the Law.

MUTILATORS OF THE FLESH

In Genesis 17, God established his covenant with Abraham by initiating a new rite called circumcision. God commanded all males eight days and older be circumcised as a sign of the covenant between God and Israel, signifying a pledge of loyalty. Circumcision is not a bad practice; however, Paul took issue with the Jews teaching circumcision as a qualification for righteousness even after Jesus became our salvation. He stressed that circumcision, as a prerequisite to salvation, was a useless cutting of the body, warning the church in Philippi to watch out for those who espoused this teaching.

**IT IS WE WHO ARE THE CIRCUMCISION, WE WHO
WORSHIP BY THE SPIRIT OF GOD**

Paul gives the true meaning of circumcision by contrasting external works with internal matters of the heart. We honor God when our worship flows from a circumcised heart, unencumbered by doubt and pride. God looks at the condition of our hearts, not the external works man tends to praise.

Romans 2:28-29 addresses the Jews that had come to believe that circumcision was a guarantee of God's favor. Take a moment to read these critical verses. What does Romans 2:28-29 tell us?

_____

_____

Circumcision is an inward work of the Holy Spirit. Only the power of the Holy Spirit can regenerate our hearts, not the law. The law reminds us of sin, but only the Holy Spirit can convict and transform.

APPLY

Ezekiel 36:26 provides better understanding. What four promises does God give us in this verse?

_____

_____

Only God can take a heart of stone and replace it with love. Grace is God's gift. As we receive it, the Holy Spirit cuts away dead things in our lives that weigh down our joy. **Transformation produces temporary pain but promises eternal gain.**

Let's end our time today by contrasting a heart of stone with a heart of flesh. Imagine holding a heart in your left hand and a stone in your right. What differences do you see and feel? What are the differences from a spiritual perspective?

Heart of Stone

_____

_____

Heart of Flesh

_____

_____

ASK

With which list did you most closely identify: the heart of stone or the heart of flesh? Ask God to help you surrender completely and soften hard places.

_____

_____

Are there "dead" areas in your life that you need to allow the Holy Spirit to cut away? If so, confess them here and cooperate with the Holy Spirit to bring transformation.

_____

_____

Prayer Challenge: *Thank You, Jesus, that when I was dead in my sins, a slave to my sin nature, You rescued me through Your death on the cross. Thank You for the gift of grace. Thank You that I am not saved or sanctified by works, but by Your blood shed for my salvation and redemption. Create in me a new heart and renew a right spirit within me.*

Paul's Résumé on File

PHILIPPIANS 3:4-6

TODAY'S VERSE

> *"If anyone else thinks he has reasons to put confidence in the flesh, I have more: circumcised on the eighth day, of the people of Israel, of the tribe of Benjamin, a Hebrew of Hebrews; in regard to the law, a Pharisee; as for zeal, persecuting the church; as for legalistic righteousness, faultless."* —Philippians 3:4-6

Paul warns his readers to watch out for people teaching righteousness obtained through works. Not only was it false teaching, but it glorified man, tempting him to find confidence in his own efforts. Paul continues by elaborating on the reasons he could boast in his own merits. He is not doing this in any way to toot his own horn, but to demonstrate that despite his pedigree and impressive résumé, he is a sinner saved by grace.

AMPLIFY

IF ANYONE ELSE THINKS HE HAS REASONS TO PUT CONFIDENCE IN THE FLESH, I HAVE MORE

Let's look at Paul's sources of identity and confidence prior to his conversion on the Damascus Road. He was a titled Jew with an extensive list of privileges and attainments. The six items included in his résumé hold significance to Jews.

1. Circumcised on the eighth day—This shows his obedience to the Covenant established with Abraham (Genesis 17:12).
2. Of the people of Israel—He was **born** a Jew, not a proselyte by his family converting.
3. Tribe of Benjamin—His Jewish roots are deep; he traces them all the way back to Joseph's younger brother Benjamin, born of the same mother, Rachel.
4. Hebrew of Hebrews—He had mastered the language, attitude, and lifestyle. Galatians 1:14 tells us that he was "extremely zealous for the traditions of his fathers."
5. Pharisee—He held the highest rank of teaching the law. While in chains and defending himself in Acts 22, he explains that he had thoroughly trained under Gamaliel (one of the best teachers in the law), was as zealous as his readers, persecuted Christians to their death (both men and women), and had entire families arrested and imprisoned. His zeal and passion for the Law were unmatched, but misplaced.
6. Legalistic righteousness—He was faultless, referring to his keeping of the law and all of its commands.

THE ROAD TO DAMASCUS

We previously traveled the Road to Damascus where Paul's destiny collided with the mystery of grace. Read Galatians 1, paying close attention to verses 13-24.

What does Paul confess that the Galatians had heard about his previous way of life?

_____

_____

What do verses 15 and 16 tell us God did?

_____

_____

The believers in Galatia were stunned to hear that the man who formerly persecuted them was now preaching the faith he had once tried to destroy. They praised God because of it. A few years earlier, this man known as "Saul" was responsible for overseeing the stoning of Stephen. Saul did all he could to make good on murderous threats against believers and take them as prisoners to Jerusalem. He went to the high priest to get letters for their arrest, and had these letters in hand on the road to Damascus.

As Saul encountered Jesus, he cowered before the light. When he got up, he was completely blind and led by the hand into Damascus. For three days, he ate and drank nothing. Meanwhile, the Lord called to Ananias in a vision and told him to go see Saul. Saul's reputation for persecuting the church prompted Ananias to express grave concern over Saul's possible false motives. Through the prayers of Ananias, God restored Saul's vision.

Saul's life would never be the same. Many years later, we find him defending himself in Acts 22. At the request of a Jewish mob, the Romans arrest him. He gives the crowd a first-hand account of what happened on the Damascus Road, admitting—with shame—to granting approval to the stoning of Stephen. Paul doesn't hide or deny his past. Rather, he puts it on display for the world to see. **Paul fervently preached the message of grace because he fully grasped the meaning of grace.**

Paul found joy in the unmerited grace of His Savior. Jesus found him. Jesus saved him. Jesus transformed him. Jesus used him. To Paul, the most important thing on his résumé was his salvation.

APPLY

FINDING OUR SOURCE

When people apply for a professional position, most submit a résumé, containing everything from education to job experience. There is nothing intrinsically wrong with education or experience. The danger comes when our source of significance and security is found in external things. Placing our worth in people, activities, and possessions creates unhealthy dependencies and a myriad of problems.

Consider what your résumé looks like. Is your confidence in your accomplishments or a list of accolades? Or, is it in Christ and what He has done for you? To help you answer those questions, write a list of some of the most important externals (people, activities, things) in your life.

_____

_____

_____

_____

How many of these could be lost or taken away?

_____

_____

The truth is, we can lose anything: our health, family, job, home, or even our life. If we find our source of identity through external means, we may crumble when they are removed. Our last name, church, education, position, status, talents...they all make it onto our identity-shaping list. I have my list, too, girls. We can't allow them to become the source of our contentment or value. If we do, we live with a conquered identity, a slave to image instead of a slave to righteousness. When our identity is found in Christ, He transforms our faulty thought patterns through the power of His Word.

Paul gives us his résumé in Philippians to make a point, *"I refuse to find my confidence in my flesh."* When we find our identity in Christ, we find joy.

ASK

How did God find you and save you? How is He using you for His glory? Girls, this is your testimony! Thank Him for how He is transforming your life! Write your Damascus Road experience below or using the page provided at the end of the Study.

_____

_____

_____

_____

_____

_____

_____

_____

The Great Reversal

PHILIPPIANS 3:7-9

TODAY'S VERSE

> *"But whatever was to my profit I now consider loss for the sake of Christ. What is more, I consider everything a loss compared to the surpassing greatness of knowing Christ Jesus my Lord, for whose sake I have lost all things. I consider them rubbish, that I may gain Christ and be found in Him, not having a righteousness of my own that comes from the law, but that which is through faith in Christ, the righteousness that comes from God and is by faith."*
> —Philippians 3:7-9

In yesterday's study, Paul gave his extensive résumé and pedigree. Today, he boldly proclaims that he considers it all nothing.

AMPLIFY

CONSIDER EVERYTHING A LOSS

Saul, miraculously transformed into the apostle Paul, moves from self-centeredness to Christ-centeredness. He no longer finds his value in his works and ability to keep the law, but in understanding God's grace. Paul takes his entire "profit column" and moves it to the "loss column."

In today's verses, he says he "considers everything a loss compared to" what?

_____

_____

Is it difficult for you to make that same statement today? Why or why not?

_____

_____

RIGHTEOUSNESS THAT COMES FROM GOD AND IS BY FAITH

True transformation take place by faith. We are righteous by faith in God. This stands in stark contrast to attaining righteousness through good works. What does righteousness really mean? "Righteous" means *to be in right standing with God*. Paul states that a right relationship with God cannot come from keeping the law but by faith in Jesus Christ. As he compares his former life and belief system to his new life in Christ, earthly things pale next to those with eternal value.

If we could gain righteousness through the law, then Christ died for nothing. God wants us to be uncompromisingly righteous through Jesus Christ. Because of this, Paul takes his lengthy and impressive résumé and throws it into the trash can. Girls, I challenge you today to be willing to do the same with your external sources of identity. Nothing else matters except Christ, our true source of joy.

What does your "everything" look like? Why is it important that we demonstrate a willingness to lose everything for Jesus' sake?

_____

_____

APPLY

1 Corinthians 1:27-30 states, "But God chose the foolish things of the world to shame the wise; God chose the weak things of the world to shame the strong. God chose the lowly things of this world and the despised things—and the things that are not—to nullify the things that are, so that no one may boast before him. It is because of him that you are in Christ Jesus, who has become for us wisdom from God—that is,

our righteousness, holiness and redemption. Therefore, as it is written: "Let the one who boasts boast in the Lord."

What does God intentionally choose to use so that man cannot boast?

_____

_____

What four things does this passage tell us Jesus has become?

_____

_____

We can rejoice today knowing it is because of Christ that we stand redeemed. We are made whole through Him. He is everything that you cannot be on your own. When you know Him and trust His character, you can rest in His power. He will complete the work He has started in your life. When we are found in Christ, shame cannot shackle us. **Grace frees us from trying to attain through the law what Christ accomplished through the cross.**

God is the author of the great reversal. When we come to Christ, we invite Him to turn our lives upside down and inside out. Whatever we might need to give up will never compare to what we gain.

ACT

Rejoice today in God's great reversal in your life! Take a moment to recount the ways God has turned your life upside down and inside out for His glory. Thank Him for the ways He is transforming your image into the image of Christ.

_____

_____

_____

_____

Living Dead

PHILIPPIANS 3:10-11

TODAY'S VERSE

"I want to know Christ and the power of his resurrection and the fellowship of sharing in his sufferings, becoming like Him in His death, and so, somehow, to attain to the resurrection from the dead." —Philippians 3:10-11

We are exploring how God brings about transformation in our life. The temporary pain we experience when we choose to die to self brings the eternal gain of knowing Christ. In Philippians 3:7-9, Paul took his entire résumé and placed it at the foot of the cross. He summed up his identity in this phrase: "I want to know Christ."

AMPLIFY

I WANT TO KNOW CHRIST

In the Old Testament, the Hebrew word for knowledge is "quot," a term used in the context of making an agreement, treaty, or truce. It literally means *to perceive, learn, understand, or experience.* In the New Testament, the Greek language uses two different words for knowledge, "oida," and "ginosko." They indicate that knowing God is a response of faith. Using these as our definitions, Paul states, "I want to **know** (enter into a treaty or agreement to learn, understand and experience as a response of faith)

Christ. I want my complete identity to be found not in external things or righteousness I can attain through works, but in the personhood, death, and resurrection of Jesus Christ."[14]

In today's verses, Paul identifies four ways in which he wants to know and become like Christ. What are they?

_____

_____

Let's explore these statements through the lens of Scripture. Search the following Scriptures and note how they paint a beautiful picture of what it means to know Christ.

APPLY

FOUR WAYS OF KNOWING CHRIST

1. **Knowing Christ in the power of His resurrection: Colossians 3:1**

_____

_____

2. **Knowing Christ in the fellowship of sharing in His sufferings: Acts 9:15-16**

_____

_____

2 Corinthians 12:9-10 says, "Therefore, in order to keep me from becoming conceited, I was given a thorn in my flesh, a messenger of Satan, to torment me. Three times I pleaded with the Lord to take it away from me. But he said to me, 'My grace is sufficient for you, for my power is made perfect in weakness.' Therefore, I will boast all the more gladly about my weaknesses, so that Christ's power may rest on me. That is why, for Christ's sake, I delight in weaknesses, in insults, in hardships, in persecutions, in difficulties. For when I am weak, then I am strong."

Why does Paul say he is not ashamed of his weaknesses?

_____

_____

How might this perspective enable Paul to live in joy?

_____

_____

What five things does Paul say he delights in for Christ's sake?

_____

_____

3. **Knowing Christ by becoming like Him in His death: Romans 6:4-13**
What does Verse 7 tell us is a wonderful result of crucifying our flesh?

_____

_____

Galatians 5:24 -25 tells us, "Those who belong to Christ Jesus have crucified the flesh with its passions and desires. Since we live by the Spirit, let us keep in step with the Spirit."

What do we need to crucify when we come to Christ?

_____

_____

4. **Knowing Christ to attain to the resurrection from the dead: Acts 24:15**

_____

_____

In Corinthians, Paul asserts that if there is no resurrection from the dead, there is no heaven and our faith is futile. Girlfriends, heaven is a guarantee of our faith. This life is not all there is. It's worth it to commit your life to knowing Christ. Not only will you experience the joy of transformation; you'll carry the hope of eternity.

ASK
What verse had the most impact on you and why?

_____

_____

Prayer Challenge: *Heavenly Father, I want to know Christ. Thank you that I belong to Christ. I am willing to crucify my flesh and my sinful nature and live by the Spirit. Holy Spirit, help me to be willing to be a partner in His sufferings. I set my heart on things above. Thank You for using temporary pain to bring eternal gain and transformation in my life. I find my joy in You.*

"INVISIBLE" / Music and Lyrics by Angela Donadio
From "This Journey"

O Lord my Rock and my Redeemer
I need to hide myself in You
Easy to find me growing weaker
It's time to disappear from view
Come transform this heart
A metamorphosis can start
To make a change in me;

(Chorus)
Make me invisible,
That's the miracle
That I am asking for
That I am less and You are more
Invisible, what a miracle
When people look at me,
You are all they see
Make me invisible.

So let this simple meditation
Be pure and blameless in Your sight
Forgive my foolish hesitations
That I so willingly invite

Come transform this heart
A metamorphosis can start
To make a change in me

(Chorus)

Let me be lost in Your presence until
I am found in Your likeness, waiting, still...

(Chorus)

"This Journey" Available on www.angeladonadio.com and iTunes

— Session 7 —

Hold Your Ground

JOY IN PERSEVERANCE
PHILIPPIANS CHAPTER 3

DAY 1 / PRESSING TOWARD THE PRIZE—CH 3:12-14

DAY 2 / FOLLOWING THE PATTERN—CH 3:15-17

DAY 3 / DISTRAUGHT OVER A DERAILED
DESTINY—CH 3:18-19

DAY 4 / DIVINE DESTINY—CH 3:18-19

DAY 5 / EYES UP—CH 3:20-21

Pressing Toward the Prize

PHILIPPIANS 3:12-14

TODAY'S VERSE

"Not that I have already obtained all this, or have already arrived at my goal, but I press on to take hold of that for which Christ Jesus took hold of me. Brothers and sisters, I do not consider myself yet to have taken hold of it. But one thing I do: Forgetting what is behind and straining toward what is ahead, I press on toward the goal to win the prize for which God has called me heavenward in Christ Jesus." —Philippians 3:12-14

Before arthritis in his elbow ended his career at the age of 30, Sandy Koufax was one of the best pitchers in Major League Baseball. From 1961-1965, he dominated the pitching mound with his explosive fastball and sharp, breaking curveball. The curveball is a type of pitch thrown with a characteristic grip and hand movement that imparts forward spin to the ball, causing it to dive in a downward path as it approaches the plate. It mimics a fastball, coming in straight to the strike zone until the very last second. Sandy Koufax's curveball was the undoing of many an unsuspecting hitter unable to adjust to the pitch in time to make contact.[15]

Life throws its share of curveballs. Perhaps you're facing one of those "I just didn't see it coming" chapters in life. You may be staring down an unexpected season of singleness or parked anxiously by the beside of a sick child. You might be struggling with financial uncertainty or dreading lab results. Whatever may be blurring your lens on life, if you know how to hold your ground, you can find joy through perseverance.

AMPLIFY

In today's passage, Paul reminds us of the importance of perseverance.

List the action verbs found in these verses. Then, we will explore them in detail.

_____

_____

OBTAINED

We studied the powerful encounter Paul, as Saul, had with Jesus Christ. It was here that Christ Jesus "took hold" of Paul. Reread Acts 9:1-18 to refresh your memory and answer the following questions.

Where did this encounter take place?

_____

_____

What was the immediate, temporal result of this encounter?

_____

_____

What was the kingdom result of this encounter?

_____

_____

ARRIVED

Paul establishes himself as a lifelong learner, acknowledging that he has not arrived at perfection. We should never stop growing by settling for mediocrity in our Christian walk. Being content with the status quo limits the capacity for God's blessing and hinders the completion of our God-given destiny. Look at the previous verses in Philippians 3 to remind yourself what Paul is referring to when he says he has not yet "obtained all this."

What has he not yet obtained?

_____

_____

What have you not yet obtained in your walk with Christ that motivates you to keep growing?

_____

_____

PRESS

Paul did not stroll leisurely through his Christian life. The word "minimalist" wasn't in his vocabulary. He pressed on intently toward the goals of knowing Christ and eternity in heaven. He refused to settle or quit. The joy before Paul was heaven, just as it was for Christ. **When we fix our eyes on the eternal, we won't become bogged down by the temporal.** Our focus is the finish line.

TAKE HOLD

When Christ Jesus took hold of Paul, his life was never the same. The King James Version translates Philippians 3:12 this way, "but I follow after, if that I may apprehend that for which also I am apprehended of Christ Jesus." "Apprehend" means *to take hold of, grasp or seize.* We previously talked about being in God's protective custody. God apprehends us with His all-surpassing grace, taking us into His custody. **Christ took hold of us at Calvary.**

How did Christ take hold of you?

_____

_____

Describe the difference you see between "pressing on" and "taking hold."

_____

_____

FORGET

Philippians 3:13 contains a powerful three-letter word that we have already discussed—*but*. After confessing that he has not taken hold of all Christ has for him, Paul points us to a critical step for finding joy.

What is the one thing he says he does?

_____

_____

What is "behind" Paul? In other words, what is in his past that he longs to forget?

_____

_____

STRAIN TOWARD WHAT IS AHEAD

Exodus 14 recounts a pivotal point in Israel's history when Moses led them out of Egypt and into the Promised Land. In Exodus 13, we learn that God did not direct them on the road through the Philistines' country although that way was shorter. God knew that to do that would put them in a place to have to fight a war and potentially cause them to retreat. Instead, He took them around by the desert road toward the Red Sea. If they were familiar with the area, they had to wonder what God was doing. To assure them, God went ahead of them as a cloud by day and a pillar of fire by night. Even with that comfort, when faced with Pharaoh's army behind them and the Red Sea in front of them, they panicked. (Honestly, I would most likely have done the same.) After encouraging them with these words, "The Lord will fight for you; you need only to be still," God instructed Moses to tell the people to move forward. To stop there would have resulted in certain death.

Joy-thirsty women, the shortest path, or the path of least resistance, is not always the way God wants you to go. No matter what, don't stop. Keep trusting His reasoning and timing. Move when He tells you to move and you'll persevere to victory.

APPLY

Paul never rested on his laurels because he wasn't finished with God's assignment. His past contained a myriad of ministry accomplishments

2d focus

as well as several clanging skeletons. Without God's grace and the help of the Holy Spirit, this kind of history would haunt most of us. For many reasons, Paul could not allow himself to live in the past.

Our past holds positive and negative experiences. Both can be difficult for us to leave behind and either has the potential to ensnare. Negative memories remind us of failures and cause us to fear the future. Likewise, we can also find ourselves stuck in our past when we fixate on positive memories. When we believe our best days are behind us, we are tempted to stop growing. We find the joy in perseverance when we let go of the past and press forward into the future. Ask God to help you forget what is behind and anticipate what is ahead. You are safely in His custody.

ASK

What is the Holy Spirit speaking to you concerning "forgetting what is behind"?

_____

_____

Write at least one reason why you cannot allow yourself to live in the past.

_____

_____

Prayer Challenge: _Holy Spirit, help me to keep my eyes fixed on You and set my heart on things above. I trust You and I release my past, present and future into Your capable hands. Thank You that my best days in You are ahead of me!_

Following the Pattern

PHILIPPIANS 3:15-17

TODAY'S VERSE

"All of us who are mature should take such a view on things. And if at some point you think differently, that too God will make clear to you. Only let us live up to what we have already attained. Join with others in following my example, brothers, and take note of those who live according to the pattern we gave you."

—Philippians 3:15-17

I suspect you'll agree that the best part of a road trip is arriving at the destination. Sure, rest stops have their share of adventures, but nothing compares to putting the car in park at the end of the journey. In today's passage, Paul reminds us that we have not yet arrived. He challenges us to continue progressing, finding the joy in perseverance.

AMPLIFY

TAKE SUCH A VIEW

To understand what Paul is referring to, we need to look at the previous verses in this chapter.

Read Philippians 3:10-11. What two goals does Paul share with us?

_____

_____

Continue reading through Verse 14. Has Paul obtained his goals?

_____

_____

These insights serve as a backdrop for today's passage. His concerns for his readers prompt him to give three important instructions. What are they?

_____

_____

When we commit to growth, we develop maturity through wisdom. In 1 Corinthians 3:1-3, Paul writes, "Brothers and sisters, I could not address you as people who live by the Spirit but as people who are still worldly—mere infants in Christ. I gave you milk, not solid food, for you were not yet ready for it. Indeed, you are still not ready. You are still worldly. For since there is jealousy and quarreling among you, are you not worldly? Are you not acting like mere humans? For when one says, 'I follow Paul,' and another, 'I follow Apollos,' are you not mere human beings?"

What does Paul mean by "I gave you milk"?

_____

_____

The believers in Corinth lacked wisdom and argued about who they liked more as a preacher—Paul or his contemporary, Apollos. Paul makes a strong distinction between the type of believer who can handle truth and those who need babying. When we don't operate in the wisdom given by the Holy Spirit, we easily become distracted and drawn off course. Look up Hebrews 5:13-14 to help underpin this spiritual principle.

Constant use means repetitive activity until it becomes learned behavior. Maturity requires us to practice discernment. We train our mind and soul to discern right from wrong and make wise choices. Failing to exercise wisdom in making decisions will affect our joy.

Do you feel you are able to handle "solid food," demonstrating a commitment to maturity? Why did you answer the way you did?

_____

_____

LIVE UP TO WHAT YOU HAVE ALREADY ATTAINED

Sometimes we are the hardest on ourselves. Take a moment and thank God for the transformation that has already taken place in your life. Living with humble gratitude for what God has done helps ensure we don't lose precious ground we have already gained. As you read Galatians 5:19-26, reflect on where you've come from.

"The acts of the flesh are obvious: sexual immorality, impurity and debauchery; idolatry and witchcraft; hatred, discord, jealousy, fits of rage, selfish ambition, dissensions, factions and envy; drunkenness, orgies, and the like. I warn you, as I did before, that those who live like this will not inherit the kingdom of God. But the fruit of the Spirit is love, joy, peace, forbearance, kindness, goodness, faithfulness, gentleness and self-control. Against such things there is no law. Those who belong to Christ Jesus have crucified the flesh with its passions and desires. Since we live by the Spirit, let us keep in step with the Spirit. Let us not become conceited, provoking and envying each other."

You belong to Christ. Your flesh doesn't have to boss you around. Through the power of the Holy Spirit, you can not only survive, but thrive.

APPLY

FOLLOW MY EXAMPLE.... LIVE ACCORDING TO THE PATTERN

Despite a having grandmother and mother who sewed beautifully, my attempts at following a pattern proved disastrous. It is not easy! It takes practice, commitment, and a steady hand. Paul asks us to follow his example, living according to the pattern he gives. As we consider what we know about Paul, many admirable character traits come to mind. Paul exemplified kingdom focus, passionate prayer, an others-oriented mindset, and contentment. Tracing the pattern of his life gives us a template for finding joy and honoring God.

Have you ever sewn something by following a pattern? What was your experience?

_____

_____

What can you extract from the example of his life that you can apply to yours?

_____

_____

ASK

Take a moment and trace a pattern of the character traits most evident in your life. Would you be confident asking other believers to follow your example? Why or why not?

_____

_____

Distraught over a Derailed Destiny

PHILIPPIANS 3:18-19

TODAY'S VERSE

"For, as I have often told you before and now say again even with tears, many live as enemies of the cross of Christ. Their destiny is destruction, their god is their stomach, and their glory is in their shame. Their mind is on earthly things." —Philippians 3:18-19

Paul is distraught over those who decided not to follow Christ. He tells us "with tears" that many failed the test of perseverance, now bound for destruction. If we are not careful, it is easy to become complacent in our Christianity, numb to the reality that people are living alienated from God and facing an eternity separated from Him. As we study today, let's ask ourselves if we share Paul's heart for the lost.

AMPLIFY

Paul gives four ways to derail a destiny. What are they?

_____

_____

_____

DESTINY IS DESTRUCTION

Can you remember a time you were in tears over someone headed for destruction? If so, what did it prompt you to do?

_____

_____

"Destruction" means the termination of something by causing it so much damage that it cannot be repaired or no longer exists; a final state. It comes from the Latin word "Exitium," meaning to tear down. Destiny doesn't derail overnight; it derails over time from destructive choices.[16]

Read Psalm 1. What three verbs do we find in the first two verses?

_____

_____

What do you notice about the progression of these three verbs?

_____

_____

What does this tell us about the power of our choices?

_____

_____

Verse 4 describes the wicked as chaff, the waste product left over after the process of threshing grain. It is inedible and worthless, simply blown away by the wind. What a sad metaphor for a life that has become unstable, losing its purpose. John 10:10 tells us that the enemy comes to kill, steal and destroy. Sin may seem fun for a season, but it will ultimately lead to your destruction and the potential destruction of the lives of others.

THEIR GOD IS THEIR STOMACH

Appetite is listed first in the things that can derail or destroy our divine destiny. Our appetites fight for instant gratification. I am not just referring to hunger pangs here, girls.

What are some potential consequences of not controlling our appetites and allowing our stomach to be our god?

_____

_____

1 Thessalonians 5:8 gives us the antidote to allowing our appetites to rule us: "But since we belong to the day, let us be sober, putting on faith and love as a breastplate, and the hope of salvation as a helmet." Another way of describing "sober" is to be "self-controlled."

What two critical areas of our body do a breastplate and a helmet cover?

_____

_____

Why do you think Paul mentions these two areas in relationship to self-control?

_____

_____

If self-control is an area of weakness for you, ask the Holy Spirit to guard your heart and mind. Confess an area you desire His help in controlling the appetites of your flesh. He will be faithful to hear and to provide all that you need.

Lord, I need greater self-control in...

_____

_____

GLORY IS IN THEIR SHAME

"Shame" means *a state of disgrace or dishonor.* Paul warns that a sign of a derailed destiny is glorifying a lifestyle that dishonors God. Psalm 4:2-3 gives us God's heart on this subject. "How long, O men, will you turn my glory into shame? How long will you love delusions and seek false gods? Know that the Lord has set apart the godly for himself; the Lord will hear when I call to him."

Think about that for a moment: God has set you apart for Himself.

How might that knowledge affect your decisions?

_____

_____

The enemy loves to use shame to keep us bound by regret. When we see ourselves through His lens—deeply valued and dearly loved—the cloak of shame is removed.

THEIR MIND IS ON EARTHLY THINGS

If you want to find joy and walk in victory, renew your mind through His Word. **Whatever you allow to dominate your thought life will ultimately shape your destiny.** We can only experience true transformation in our lives through the renewing of our mind. Information requires application if we want to see transformation.

APPLY

MIND MAKEOVER

Our thoughts are like a recording that plays over and over in our mind. Until we change the recording, we won't experience true joy and deliverance from shame. We can't change our past, but we can allow God to sweep our minds clean from the destructive thoughts that threaten our future. God is in the business of destiny reversal. Past decisions do not have to determine your divine destiny. These two Scriptures promise the joy you receive when you commit to a mind makeover.

Romans 12:2—"Do not conform to the pattern of this world, but be transformed by the renewing of your mind. Then you will be able to test and approve what God's will is—his good, pleasing and perfect will."

Mind Makeover: Joy-thirsty women, you receive the ability to understand His perfect will for your life.

Ephesians 4:22-24—"You were taught, with regard to your former way of life, to put off your old self, which is being corrupted by its deceitful desires; to be made new in the attitude of your minds; and to put on the new self, created to be like God in true righteousness and holiness."

Mind Makeover: *Joy-thirsty women, you get to trade in your old self and receive a new attitude that reflects the beauty of Christ.*

Identify an area of your thought life that needs a mind makeover. Allow any damaging thoughts to be swept clean by the renewing power of grace.

_____

_____

ASK

Do you see yourself as deeply valued and dearly loved? If not, what is obscuring the lens of how God views you?

_____

_____

Prayer Challenge: *Holy Spirit, develop Your fruit in my life, especially self-control. Help me to guard my heart and my mind. Thank You that You hold my destiny in Your hands. Help me to live a lifestyle that brings honor and glory to You.*

Divine Destiny

PHILIPPIANS 3:18-19

TODAY'S VERSE

"For, as I have often told you before and now say again even with tears, many live as enemies of the cross of Christ. Their destiny is destruction, their god is their stomach, and their glory is in their shame. Their mind is on earthly things." —Philippians 3:18-19

———————————————

Paul outlined the path that leads to a derailed and destroyed destiny. This is not God's plan for His daughters. He has an amazing, divine destiny for you!

AMPLIFY

"Destiny" means *overall circumstances or condition in life*. Let's take another pass at the same verses we just studied contrasting a destroyed destiny with a divine destiny. I want us to examine three areas that will determine your destiny: body, mind, and soul. Having God's perspective will help you hold your ground when temptation strikes.

Let's draw contrasts between the two destinies below. I have started some thoughts for you, and I would like you to add to the lists. Try to be as personal and specific as you can, adding your own experiences.

BODY = APPETITE

Divine destiny is marked by self-control

I hunger for God more than anything

_____

_____

Derailed destiny is marked by lack of boundaries

I easily give into sin

_____

_____

MIND = ATTITUDE

Divine destiny is renewed and transformed

The Word of God shapes my thoughts

_____

_____

Derailed destiny is unguarded and unbridled

My thought patterns are destructive and unproductive

_____

_____

SOUL/SPIRIT = AMBITION

Divine destiny is surrendered

I have freedom in my relationships because I am walking in forgiveness

_____

_____

Derailed destiny is selfish

I am trapped by painful emotions and pride

_____

_____

I pray you allowed the Holy Spirit to tenderly shine His flashlight into intimate places of your heart. Use that list as a catalyst to answer the questions at the end of today's homework.

APPLY

Temptation presents itself in many forms with one goal: to derail your divine destiny. We are more apt to succumb to the pitfalls of appetite, attitude or ambition when we are hungry, angry, lonely or tired. The "HALT" acronym is widely taught to help recognize red flags and avert needless tragedy.[17]

Learning to "HALT" when you feel weak in one or more area shields your integrity and protects your destiny.

H—Hungry
A—Angry
L—Lonely
T—Tired

1 Corinthians 10:13 tells us, "No temptation has overtaken you except what is common to mankind. And God is faithful; he will not let you be tempted beyond what you can bear. But when you are tempted, he will also provide a way out so that you can endure it." God always provides you with the strength you need to hold your ground against the enemy's schemes. Succumbing to temptation will swallow your joy. Don't let it happen, beautiful girls; you are worth fighting for. The next time temptation hovers dangerously close to your divine destiny, stop and consider the potential ramifications of a decision before you act.

Decisions determine destiny. A destiny is really another way of saying a destination. If destiny is a destination, and decisions determine destiny, it is important to look at your decisions. They reveal where you are going and where you want to go. If your desire is to walk in daily obedience, you will arrive at your God-given destiny. Our minute-by-minute, hourly, daily, monthly, and yearly choices ultimately lead us to our destination. Using the Word of God as your manual for daily living will keep you out of temptation's clutches and in God's absolute best.

ASK

Perhaps you are making a critical choice or decision now. If so, apply these questions to your current decision-making process and write your thoughts in the space provided for you. Consider copying these questions before you answer them as a tool for future decisions. You can also use them to help guide a spouse, child, or friend toward a godly decision.

DECISION MAKING GUIDE

Where do you want to go in life? In what ways do you want your life to look different than it does right now? Write with detail.

_____

_____

Do your goals, plans, dreams, and aspirations line up with the Word of God? Be specific and honest. If they don't, they aren't a part of God's divine destiny for you.

_____

_____

What is one step can you make right now toward a God-directed goal?

_____

_____

What is the potential outcome, cost, or fruit of making this decision? (A sin of commission is willfully committing an action you know to be contrary to the Word of God).

_____

_____

Prayer Challenge: _God, I thank You for redeeming my past. Thank You for revealing Yourself to me in my present. Thank You for rejoicing with me over my future. I choose to love you with all my heart, all my mind and all my strength. Receive glory from my life. Amen._

Eyes Up!

PHILIPPIANS 3:20-21

TODAY'S VERSE

"But our citizenship is in heaven. And we eagerly await a Savior from there, the Lord Jesus Christ, who, by the power that enables him to bring everything under his control, will transform our lowly bodies so that they will be like his glorious body."
—Philippians 3:20-21

Grocery lists. Soccer games. Bible study. Endless meetings. Piano lessons. Piles of laundry. Sound familiar? Daily living can obscure our vision of the eternal. We find joy as we are reminded that we are citizens of heaven.

AMPLIFY

BUT OUR CITIZENSHIP IS IN HEAVEN

The process of becoming a United States citizen is arduous, often requiring a hefty amount of patience. As we wait for our ultimate citizenship in heaven, Paul encourages us to keep our eyes fixed on eternity.

What is the tiny but weighty word at the beginning of our passage?

_____

_____

In previous verses, Paul described the characteristics of a person who lives as an enemy of the cross. Now, he draws the distinction between unbelievers and the believers he is addressing. Rather than merely living for earthly pleasure and instant gratification, Paul reaffirms that his citizenship is heaven.

What does John 17:14-15 tell us about our citizenship?

_____

_____

This is not our home. Amid the perils of war, famine, disease and adversity, remember that we are just passing through. Keeping a heavenly perspective adjusts the lens through which we view life.

EAGERLY AWAIT A SAVIOR

Satisfying our selfish desires brings immediate gratification but dire consequences. Focusing on the promise of eternity in heaven allows us to resist our flesh and embrace delayed gratification. If we operate in the expectation that Jesus is coming again to take His bride to heaven, we will live with our "eyes up."

Describe a time that you eagerly awaited for an event or a situation to take place. What were the details surrounding the event and what did you feel during this time?

_____

_____

What makes it difficult to keep our eyes fixed on heaven and eagerly await our Savior's return?

_____

_____

WHO BY THE POWER THAT ENABLES HIM TO BRING EVERYTHING UNDER HIS CONTROL

In the Garden of Gethsemane, Jesus obeyed His Father by resisting temptation from both Satan and His own humanity. Hebrews 5:8 tells us that Jesus learned obedience through what He suffered. It is easier to obey if we remember that our Heavenly Father has everything under His control. We previously studied John 13 where Jesus washed the disciples' feet. Verse 3 shares,

> *"Jesus knew that the Father had put all things under his power, and that he had come from God and was returning to God."*

Jesus understood His destiny. In John 14, Jesus taught His disciples how to demonstrate love through obedience. Take a moment to read chapter 14 and reflect on this passage.

What does Jesus tell them He is going to do?

_____

_____

What does verse 15 say we will do if we love Him?

_____

_____

OBEDIENCE RELEASES GOD'S BLESSING

God can bring everything under His control. When we believe this truth, we can trust Him completely and stay centered in His will. Perhaps a pressing situation is causing you to worry. In what way does it reassure your heart to know God is able to bring everything under His control?

_____

_____

HE WILL TRANSFORM OUR LOWLY BODIES SO THAT THEY WILL BE LIKE HIS GLORIOUS BODY

I don't know about you, girls, but I cannot wait for a new body. Goodbye aches and pains; hello heaven! God's power is transformational. The ultimate change comes when our earthly bodies no longer hold us captive. We will become like Christ.

154

APPLY

In 1887, John H. Sammis penned the words to what became one of the most beloved hymns of all time, "Trust and Obey." Such simple words, but so difficult to do.

When we walk with the Lord in the light of His Word,
What a glory He sheds on our way!
While we do His good will, He abides with us still,
And with all who will trust and obey.

(Refrain)
Trust and obey, for there's no other way
To be happy in Jesus, but to trust and obey.

Not a shadow can rise, not a cloud in the skies,
But His smile quickly drives it away;
Not a doubt or a fear, not a sigh or a tear,
Can abide while we trust and obey.

Not a burden we bear, not a sorrow we share,
But our toil He doth richly repay;
Not a grief or a loss, not a frown or a cross,
But is blessed if we trust and obey.

But we never can prove the delights of His love
Until all on the altar we lay;
For the favor He shows, for the joy He bestows,
Are for them who will trust and obey.

Then in fellowship sweet we will sit at His feet,
Or we'll walk by His side in the way;
What He says we will do, where He sends we will go;
Never fear, only trust and obey.

What is one way the words of this hymn minister to you?

_____

_____

No matter what is happening around you, keep your eyes up. Remember, this life is a blink compared to eternity. Joy-thirsty women, you can stand your ground and find the joy in perseverance. God is preparing a place for you. Hold on, girls. Heaven is coming.

ASK

What are you most looking forward to about heaven?

_____

_____

"NAIL-PIERCED HANDS" / Music and Lyrics by Angela Donadio
From "It's A New Day"

Broken, wounded, misunderstood,
Rejected, abandoned, hung on a piece of wood,
The Son of God, the Great I am
Became the substitute for man
And Jesus understands when I'm
Broken, wounded, misunderstood,
Rejected, abandoned, desperate to see the good,
It's in that place You call my name
Tell me again You took my pain
So I can understand;

(Chorus)
It is in Your nail-pierced hands that hold me
I know You love me and that gives me strength to stand
It is Your nail-pierced hands that hold me
Your mercy came and drew a line in the sand
With Your nail-pierced hands.

Mended, forgiven, loved as I am
Accepted, reborn, and free to give again
The Son of God, the Great I am
Became the substitute for man
And Jesus understands

(Bridge)
There have been times when I felt devastated, left for dead,
Hopelessly lost and wondering what I'd face in days ahead,
But in those moments when I questioned how I'd make it through,
My hope, my strength, my source, I found it all in You.

(Chorus)
It is Your nail-pierced hands that hold me,
I know You love me and that gives me strength to stand
It is Your nail-pierced hands that hold me
Your mercy came and drew a line in the sand
With Your nail-pierced hands.

"It's A New Day" Available on www.angeladonadio.com and iTunes

— Session 8 —

Think About It

JOY IN VICTORY
PHILIPPIANS CHAPTER 4

DAY 1 / STAND FIRM—CH 4:1

DAY 2 / A WOMAN OF INFLUENCE—CH 4:2-3

DAY 3 / THE PROMISE OF PEACE—CH 4:4-7

DAY 4 / DECORATING OTHERS—CH 4:8

DAY 5 / A GOOD REPORT—CH 4:8

Stand Firm

PHILIPPIANS 4:1

TODAY'S VERSE

"Therefore, my brothers, you whom I love and long for, my joy and crown, that is how you should stand firm in the Lord, dear friends!"
—Philippians 4:1

I am one of over half a billion people worldwide who use the social media site Facebook. I am prompted to update my personal profile status by answering a single question: "What's on your mind?" My answers have ranged from weighing in on social issues to wondering why there isn't a Schlotzsky's within a 100-mile radius of my house. As we come to the last chapter of this short but rich book, Philippians, I would like to make the same inquiry. "Joy-thirsty women, what's on your mind?"

The brain is a wonder. Experts estimate that we think between 50,000–70,000 thoughts a day. Our thoughts are influenced by internal dialogue and external factors including opinions, judgements and feelings. Our minds are under constant attack from our own thoughts and from the lies of the enemy. Add to that the steady stream of garbage from media outlets and an overstimulated, secular culture, and we've got ourselves an all-out war. However, we can find joy in victory when we win the battle for our thoughts.[18]

AMPLIFY

What's on Paul's mind today? The answer should come as no surprise: people.

Who is Paul referring to in today's verse? (Think back to previous weeks of lessons.)

_____

_____

What two verbs does Paul use to describe his feelings for them?

_____

_____

What two nouns does he use to describe the people he loves in this verse?

_____

_____

What do the last two words tell us about his relationship with them?

_____

_____

Paul dedicated his life to the cause of Christ and to the salvation of others. Committed to relationship, people are his life's work on display. With a plethora of choices clamoring for the investment of his time and energies, Paul valued people over position, property, or power.

What or who are you investing yourself into? What or who is your "joy and crown"?

_____

_____

STAND FIRM

Although today's verse begins a new chapter, it is a continuation of his previous exhortation in Philippians 3. Remember when we read a "therefore" in a verse, we need to know what it is there for. Look back at Chapter 3:19-21 and see to what Paul is referring.

What enables us to stand firm?

_____

_____

APPLY

Let's unpack what it means to stand firm.

KNOWING GOD'S CHARACTER HELP US TO STAND FIRM

God is all-powerful, and His character is unchanging. He will enable you to walk in victory even during the fiercest storm. The enemy will attempt to rob you of your joy and destroy your efforts to remain strong in the Lord. However, as you continue to build yourself up through His Word, you will grow in your understanding of God.

What do the following passages from Psalms show us about the nature and character of God? Note what stands firm in each Scripture.

Psalm 33:11

_____

_____

Psalm 89:2

_____

_____

Psalm 93:5

_____

_____

Psalm 119:89

_____

_____

Why does knowing more about your Heavenly Father enable you to place greater trust in Him?

_____

_____

SCRIPTURE TEACHES US TO STAND FIRM

We previously studied the armor of God in Ephesians 6, a vital component to standing firm during difficulty and temptation.

Read Ephesians 6:10-18 again and count how many times Paul uses the word "stand."

_____

_____

Paul describes both an aggressive offensive and defensive posture. We can remain immovable in the face of the enemy's assault because of God's protection. However, we must use the weapons He provides. If you want to live in victory, don't just put them on, leave them on.

You were created to be an overcomer. Chew on the following passages, digesting the importance of standing firm.

"Therefore, my dear brothers, stand firm. Let nothing move you. Always give yourselves fully to the work of the Lord, because you know that your labor in the Lord is not in vain." —1 Corinthians 15:58

"It is for freedom that Christ has set us free. Stand firm, then, and do not let yourselves be burdened again by a yoke of slavery." — Galatians 5:1

"If you do not stand firm in your faith, you will not stand at all." —Isaiah 7:9

Which Scripture speaks to you most today?

_____

_____

WHAT WE RECEIVE BY STANDING FIRM

We have explored how we stand firm. Let's conclude today by looking at what we receive when we remain unwavering in our faith. You may also choose to look up additional references using your concordance or online Bible search engine for the words "stand firm." Add any other benefits you find in Scripture.

KEY SCRIPTURE	WHAT WE RECEIVE BY STANDING FIRM
Exodus 14:13-14	*Deliverance*
2 Chronicles 20:15-17	
Psalm 40:2	*Trust/Confidence*
Psalm 20:7-8	
Luke 21:19	*Eternal Life*
Other....	

ASK

The Word of God is inexhaustible, alive, and active. I encourage you to continue applying the truth of His Word long after you have completed this study. It will transform your mind and give you the tools you need to live in victory, including a new lens on your perspective.

Conclude today by writing the following verse in the space provided. Make it personal by replacing each bold phrase with your own name. This is your promise. God will enable you to stand firm.

*"Now it is God who makes **both us and you** stand firm in Christ. He anointed **us**, set his seal of ownership on us, and put his Spirit in **our** hearts as a deposit, guaranteeing what is to come,"* —2 Corinthians 1:21-22

A Woman of Influence

PHILIPPIANS 4:2-3

TODAY'S VERSE

"I plead with Euodia and I plead with Syntyche to agree with each other in the Lord. Yes, and I ask you, loyal yokefellow, help these women who have contended at my side in the cause of the Gospel, along with Clement and the rest of my fellow workers, whose names are in the book of life." —Philippians 4:2-3

In Mark 6, Jesus used a young boy's lunch to feed over five thousand famished listeners. Placed in His hands, five loaves and two fish miraculously became a meal replete with baskets of leftovers. Jesus is a master at multiplication; however, He doesn't do division.

God hates disunity. The concept of unity is also important to Paul. This is the second mention of it in four short chapters. Although today's passage does not contain the *word* "unity," it is the primary theme. We previously studied Scripture to see three critical results of unity: power, blessing, and a witness to the lost. Women, we can't find joy without it.

AMPLIFY

Who are the two women Paul is pleading with in today's passage?

_____

_____

What is he pleading with them to do?

_____

_____

How thrilling to discover that you are included in the sacred pages of Scripture! How equally tragic to find that this is your entry. We don't know much about these two women, including their background or the source of their conflict. However, we do learn one important detail about their relationship with Paul. They are fellow believers who have worked closely with him in his missionary efforts. Women surrounded Jesus' ministry, and they surround the ministry of Paul. Priscilla was one of the New Testament's leading women.

What does 1 Corinthians 16:19-20 tell us about Aquila and Priscilla?

_____

_____

Let's go back to the women of the hour. What does the end of today's passage tell us about Euodia and Syntyche?

_____

_____

These are Christian women in some form of leadership in the church in Philippi. Yet, their inability to get along has reached the ears of Paul in Rome. Yikes! It is probable that Paul knew of other disagreements. Why do you think Paul singled these two women out by name, pleading with them to reconcile their differences?

_____

_____

How I wish I could hear some of your answers. Let's explore this together.

APPLY

RELATIONAL CONFLICT

The question of the week is, "What's on your mind?" Sadly, many social media posts describe challenges in relationships. A leading joy-killer is relational conflict. Even Paul was not exempt from it, and he includes this passage for our benefit. First, Paul has already shown us how dearly he loves the people of Philippi. It would grieve him to hear that two of his key leaders have not been able to smooth out their differences.

What might have kept them from resolving their conflict? (Think of instances where you have been involved in relational struggles to help facilitate your answers).

_____
_____
_____
_____

Matthew 18:15-17 gives us the Biblical steps for handling conflict. What are they?

_____
_____

We serve a relational God; He has designed us that way. Women are relational; yet, this can lead to emotionally charged conversations and offenses. **Wise women guard their hearts and bridle their tongues.** Conflict takes place when there is a clash of expectations between two people.

How have you seen that to be true?

_____
_____

We must commit to resolving disagreements in a healthy, Biblical way. Regrettably, far too many conflicts in churches involve women. Gossip can be both a byproduct of conflict and the source of conflict. Proverbs 16:28 tells us, "A perverse person stirs up conflict, and a gossip separates close friends." Gossip is no small thing. Romans 1:28-32 lists greed, murder, arrogance and God-haters alongside—gulp—gossip. The words in verse 31 are profound: "They have no understanding, no fidelity, no love, and no mercy." Women, let this not be said of us! Sometimes, relationships require adjustments to be healthy and God-honoring. We are not responsible for the actions of others, but we are responsible for our reactions.

INFLUENCE

The second reason Paul included the story of Euodia and Syntyche is because they held positions of influence within the church of Philippi. To "influence" something is *to have an effect or have the power to sway*. **The measure of a leader is their ability to influence others.** Women are powerful influencers. We tend to set the emotional tone in a home or a church. If women are cold, a home or church has the potential to be cold. Likewise, if women are warm, their environment reflects their demeanor.

CHECKLIST FOR HEALTHY RELATIONSHIPS

Unresolved relational conflict pickpockets your joy and steals your victory. You will be a woman of influence in the kingdom of God as you honor these commitments in your relationships:

- Keep lines of communication open and clear. This contains the enemy and exposes his strategies.
- Submit to spiritual authority and walk in humility.
- Refuse to "take up another's offense" and resolve conflict according to Matthew 18.
- Develop the ability to be a Spirit-led listener. Listen for three things: what is being said, what is being left unsaid, and the underlining root cause.

ASK

Reflect on your personal relationships, evaluating any that harbor unresolved relational conflict. Allow the Holy Spirit to speak to you about His will for your life in this area.

If gossip is an area of struggle for you, confess that to the Lord. Ask Him where you may need to repent. Consider what actions the Lord would have you take if gossip has marred or damaged someone else's reputation.

_____

_____

_____

_____

Prayer Challenge: *Holy Spirit, I want my life to honor You in every way. I commit myself to You and Your Word. Help me to be committed to relationship unity and be the woman of influence You have created me to be.*

The Promise of Peace

PHILIPPIANS 4:4-7

TODAY'S VERSE

"Rejoice in the Lord always. I will say it again: Rejoice! Let your gentleness be evident to all. The Lord is near. Do not be anxious about anything, but in everything, by prayer and petition, with thanksgiving, present your requests to God. And the peace of God, which transcends all understanding, will guard your hearts and your minds in Christ Jesus." —Philippians 4:4-7

Nestled between Paul's appeal for unity in verses 2 and 3 and his request for gentleness in verse 4, is a reminder to rejoice in the Lord. It is more like a command. We have a vital part to play if we want to live in joy. Today's passage gives us even more insight as to how this is possible. It contains five instructions and two promises. List them below:

Instructions:

_____

_____

_____

_____

Promises:

_____

_____

_____

_____

AMPLIFY

We are going to focus our attention first on the five instructions (commands) Paul gives us.

REJOICE IN THE LORD ALWAYS. I WILL SAY IT AGAIN: REJOICE

It requires discipline to stay in an attitude of joy. How often does Paul tell us to rejoice?

_____

_____

He even repeats the command twice in one verse. God gives us the ability through the power of the Holy Spirit to rejoice in the Lord in all circumstances.

What does James 1:2-4 tell us about joy?

_____

_____

What must finish its work in our lives?

_____

_____

"Perseverance" means *persistent determination, tenacity, stability, firmness, patience, singleness of purpose.* When our faith is tested, we develop perseverance and become mature in Christ. God is not asking us to rejoice in the trial itself. He is asking us to rejoice in the result of the trial. God can use trials in your life to make you mature and complete, lacking nothing. Those are amazing results. That is something to rejoice about!

How would your life look different if you were mature and complete in Christ, not lacking anything?

_____

_____

LET YOUR GENTLENESS BE EVIDENT TO ALL

2 Corinthians 10:1 tells us that gentleness is a character trait of Jesus. He trusted the Father completely, (as should we), enabling Him to walk in gentleness. Galatians 5 lists this trait as a fruit or evidence of the Holy Spirit working in our lives. We must make a willful decision to cooperate with the Spirit to produce His fruit in us. When we do, everyone sees the fruit of gentleness in us.

DO NOT BE ANXIOUS ABOUT ANYTHING

This, my friends, is a challenging command. Say it aloud a couple of times. It can be difficult to avoid feeling anxious or fearful, especially when we are "in the waiting room of God." **When we are waiting, God is working.** He wants us to learn to wait without anxiety and to trust Him. He knows that we will wrestle at times with worry and fear. Thankfully, He tells us what to do with our anxiety.

According to 1 Peter 5:7, what should we do?

_____

_____

Why are we able to do this?

_____

_____

Reframe worry as a negative form of prayer. It is completely counterproductive. Anxiety and prayer are two formidable opposing forces in the battlefield of our mind. Each day, anxiety and worry face off against gratitude and trust. God wants us to give us the victory. Staying in a state of internal turmoil competes with our quest to live in joy. The last instruction in today's passage gives us the antidote to worry, "In everything, by prayer and petition, with thanksgiving, present your requests to God." Women, we can live in peace instead of anxiety.

What is one thing you can thank the Lord for today?

_____

_____

Which instruction in today's lesson is most challenging to you and why? Ask the Holy Spirit to help you in this area.

_____

_____

APPLY

THE PROMISES OF GOD

These commands challenge us, but these two promises comfort us:

- "The Lord is near"
- "And the peace of God, which transcends all understanding, will guard your heart and minds in Christ Jesus."

The peace of God stands guard over our hearts and our minds. We become anxious when we feel the need to guard ourselves against threats, real or perceived, in the attempt to protect ourselves from pain or abuse. In doing so, we resist the Lord's peace by not trusting His protection and care. God is your protector. He offers you His peace as a guard over your thoughts (mind) and emotions (heart). Living within the boundaries of God's Word is part of God's blueprint for peace. So often, we forfeit the peace of God in our lives due to our own stubbornness and poor choices. When we resist submitting to God's authority, we attack the parameters He has established for our good. Peace of mind is a reward for living a lifestyle that honors God and respects the boundaries of His Word.

ASK

Is there an area of your life where you are not honoring "God-designed boundaries"?

_____

_____

If so, what steps do you want to make to live in the fullness of God's joy and peace for your life?

_____

_____

Joy-thirsty women, it is possible to live in peace, both internally with ourselves and externally with others. We can live in joy regardless of circumstances if we trust that God has our best intentions at heart. Let me leave you with a powerful verse we previously studied as a reminder that the peace of God offers us supernatural protection. Personalize it. You are loved and protected by God!

"You will keep in perfect peace him whose mind is steadfast, because he trusts in You," —Isaiah 26:3

"You will keep me in perfect peace. My mind is steadfast and I trust in You."

_____

_____

_____

_____

_____

_____

Decorating Others

PHILIPPIANS 4:8

TODAY'S VERSE

"Finally, brothers, whatever is true, whatever is noble, whatever is right, whatever is pure, whatever is lovely, whatever is admirable--if anything is excellent or praiseworthy—think about such things."
—Philippians 4:8

Paul understood the influence our thoughts have on our lives. What we allow to occupy our thought life will determine our beliefs, our actions, and our destinies.

Read what Paul says about this in 2 Corinthians 10:5.

What are we to take captive?

What are we to do with them?

I want to challenge you today to think about your thoughts. As we walk through our study, I will ask you to answer questions about what you are allowing to take up residence in your mind. In Psalm 19:14, David prays, "May the words of my mouth and the meditation of my heart be pleasing in your sight, O Lord, my Rock and my Redeemer." Listening to the words you speak will reveal the nature of thought life and the overflow of your heart.

We cannot just change our words; we must change the underlining root and belief system behind them. Our words reveal where we are struggling with a critical spirit, fear, or pride. They can also disclose a deficiency in thankfulness or mercy. What should occupy our thoughts? Philippians 4:8 gives us the answers. We will divide this verse into two days of study. Don't rush. Allow the Holy Spirit to speak to you about setting your thoughts apart for His glory.

AMPLIFY

THINK ABOUT SUCH THINGS

Women, what we think about matters. You may have walked through life believing that you have no control over your thought life. As we have seen in Scripture, that simply is not true. The Holy Spirit can sanctify our thought life, setting it apart, making it holy and pleasing to the Lord. We have choices about what occupies our thoughts. In today's passage, Philippians 4:8, Paul lists eight characteristics of a godly thought life. What are they?

_____

_____

_____

_____

TRUE

Our thoughts must center on truth. Satan is the author of deceit. He will do anything to keep you bound and confused, including using lies about God, about you, and about others. You will experience victory when you ask God to uproot any lie from the enemy that you may have believed, replacing them with the truth of God's Word. For many years, my struggle with perfectionism cemented the lie that I was never good enough for God to love me. By applying the salve of His Word to my broken places, truth uprooted the lie.

Is there a lie in your life that the Holy Spirit needs replace with His truth?

_____

_____

NOBLE

To be "noble" is to be of elevated character. A noble woman is worthy of honor or respect. Ruth, the heroine of the book that bears her name, is richly blessed by God because of her noble character. **God cannot take us where our character cannot keep us.** Crisis in leadership takes place when someone's charisma is greater than his or her character. Character is who we really are when no one is looking, and it matters to God.

What thoughts and actions elevate character?

_____

_____

RIGHT/JUST

Righteousness is a characteristic of God. He gives us the backbone to do the right thing by making choices that reflect His heart. You can't wait until you're smack dab in the middle of a situation to decide whether you will choose righteousness. You'll have to make up your mind in advance to honor God if you want to live victoriously in joy. Psalm 25:9 says, "He guides the humble in what is right and teaches them His way." He will empower you to make wise choices if you stay humble and teachable.

God is a just God, and He asks us to do the right thing, even when it is hard. As a dear friend has said to me on numerous occasions, *"It is better to* **do** *right than to* **be** *right."* Let justice be God's domain. When we are hurt or offended, it is tempting for us to take justice into our own hands. We do this in many ways, such as secretly wanting the other person to suffer for wounding us or withholding forgiveness.

Is there a situation with an individual where you have taken justice into your own hands? If so, confess that here and let justice be God's domain. He will reward you for your righteousness.

_____

_____

PURE

Psalm 51 is one of the most gut-wrenching passages in Scripture. King David penned this passionate plea for God's mercy after the prophet Nathan confronted him about his adulterous relationship with Bathsheba. Riddled with guilt and regret, David pours out his anguish to a merciful God. In verses 10-12, David asks God to create a clean heart in him, pleading for God's presence to remain and his joy to be restored. David knew the sustaining power of joy. A pure heart is a prerequisite to living in true joy. When we make choices that are consistent with the Word of God, we will have a clear conscience and peace of mind.

What does Matthew 5:8 say about the pure in heart?

_____

_____

LOVELY

Lovely in, lovely out. To refer to something as "lovely" is to say it is *beautiful and worthy of honor*. Be selective in what you allow into your spirit. As a musician, I have seen the powerful effect music has on people, especially spiritually. What we listen to and watch has a dramatic effect on our thoughts. We have the option to feed our spirit or our flesh. Whichever you choose to feed will thrive.

APPLY

Joy-thirsty women, determine that your thoughts will reflect the Word of God. Thoughts form beliefs and beliefs disclose themselves through words and actions. You are not powerless over your thought life. You are a woman of influence. Use that influence today to decorate others with your words.

ASK

Think of one person you influence through your presence. How can you decorate their life with your words this week?

_____

_____

A Good Report

PHILIPPIANS 4:8

TODAY'S VERSE

"Finally, brothers, whatever is true, whatever is noble, whatever is right, whatever is pure, whatever is lovely, whatever is admirable—if anything is excellent or praiseworthy—think about such things."
—Philippians 4:8

We are studying the eight criteria for a godly thought life presented in Philippians 4:8. Today we focus our attention on "admirable, excellent, or praiseworthy." Our thoughts need to emphasize things that are worth admiring and of good report. Unfortunately, we are quick to reflect on and report the negative. Bad news sells. Yet, even when times are tough, we can choose to give a good report. This does not mean we disregard the facts or deny truth. As we practiced in an earlier exercise, we can place our situation under the covering of God's character. We can decide to trust God in all things at all times to be our protector, provider, and deliverer.

AMPLIFY

For today's lesson, I would like us to look at the King James translation. Philippians 4:8 states, "whatsoever things are of good report; if there be any virtue, and if there be any praise, think on these things." The original Greek word used for "of good report" is "euphemos," meaning, "well reported of." We will study Numbers chapters 13 and 14 to see a powerful demonstration of the value of a good report. This passage of Scripture recounts a moment in Israel's history when their lack of faith proved to be a turning point for the nation.

OF GOOD REPORT

In Numbers 13 and 14, we see Moses leading the Israelites out of years of slavery and bondage in Egypt and into Canaan, the land that God had promised them. Please read both chapters in their entirety, paying close attention to the reports of Joshua and Caleb.

FROM NUMBERS 13:

What did God ask Moses to do?

_____
_____

What did Moses ask the leaders to do?

_____
_____

How many days did the leaders spy out the land?

_____
_____

Despite its rich soil and abundance of fruit, ten leaders came back and gave the following report: "But the people who live there are powerful and the cities are fortified and very large. We even saw descendants of Anak there. The Amalekites live in the Negev; the Hittites, Jebusites and Amorites live in the hill country; and the Canaanites live near the sea and along the Jordan."

The descendants of Anak were relatives of Goliath, from the Philistines. 1 Samuel 17 records the story of Goliath, the 9'9" giant leader of the Philistine army. He taunted the people of Israel for weeks until a young shepherd boy named David killed him with a slingshot, a stone, and Goliath's own sword. In the natural, the Israelite army faced impossible odds against these strong military contingents and fortified cities.

In Chapter 13:30, what does Caleb do to the people?

_____

_____

What report does Caleb give to Moses?

_____

_____

This stands in sharp contrast to the account from the other ten spies. They sketched a land filled with giants, superior weaponry and insurmountable walls. What emotions likely drove them to bring back a negative report?

_____

_____

FROM NUMBERS 14:

What do the people of Israel do all night in response to their bad report? Notice how quickly the Israelites disintegrate into chaos.

What a tragic mistake these ten leaders made. In a matter of moments, all because of their words, the Israelites turned their backs on their leaders, God, and the Promised Land. But every good story needs a hero, and ours has two. Who brings a good report?

_____

_____

List at least three elements of their report:

_____

_____

What a difference! Remember, the 12 leaders sent as spies all saw the same thing but only Caleb and Joshua brought back a report full of faith in God. What does God say about Caleb in Numbers 14:24?

_____

_____

The rest of Chapter 14 communicates the terrible consequences of the leaders' choice to spread the negative account among the people. In response to the Israelites' complaints and lack of faith in God, God says the following in verse 34: "For forty years—one year for each of the forty days you explored the land—you will suffer for your sins and know what it is like to have Me against you."

Women, this chapter gives us the reason the Israelites spent forty years wandering and dying in a desert. The journey from Egypt to Canaan should have taken forty days. Fear and frustration gripped the Israelites until they rose up in rebellion against their leaders and against God. Their trust in God crumbled to the ground at the words from faithless spies. In punishment, an entire generation died in the wilderness, including the leaders that spread a bad report. From that generation, God allowed only Joshua and Caleb to enter the Promised Land. Years later, Joshua succeeded Moses as the leader of the nation of Israel. His character, tested in adversity, proved noble and worthy of honor. In Joshua 14, Joshua led the Israelites to victory and possession of the Promised Land. Read this passage of Scripture to hear the miraculous ending to Caleb's story.

How old is Caleb? _____

How does he describe the events that took place 40 years earlier (from Numbers 13 and 14)?

_____

_____

What does Joshua give him?

_____

_____

In the King James translation, Caleb states: "Now therefore give me this mountain, whereof the Lord spake in that day; for thou heardest in that day how the Anakims were there, and that the cities were great and fenced: if so be the Lord will be with me, then I shall be able to drive them out, as the Lord said." The NIV translation states, "Now give me this hill country that the Lord promised me that day." This story inspired part of the lyric for "It's a New Day," the title track of my second album:

"Some see the giants, I see a mighty God. Give me the mountain my name is written on."

God always blesses our obedience and faith. Forty years after Caleb chose to place his faith in God rather than cower in fear, he received his inheritance. Women, what a powerful example we have in Joshua and Caleb of making every thought obedient to Christ. That fateful day recorded in Numbers 13 and 14 determined the destiny of two great men, ten fearful spies, and an entire nation.

Paul includes "of good report" for a good reason. What might have happened to the ten other spies and the nation of Israel if they had brought back a good report?

_____

_____

APPLY

It is not what we see that determines our faith, but what we know about God that makes the difference. Caleb and Joshua saw everything the other spies saw, but they believed the Lord would deliver them. Our words affect our destiny and the destiny of the people around us. Perhaps you're scouting the terrain ahead and the odds seem stacked against you. Bills look like giants and the walls between you and a loved one seem too monstrous to tackle. **Believe God for the best possible outcome.** Begin to thank God for how He is going to bring you through it and how He is going to reveal Himself to you. Start by offering this simple prayer from a fragile heart: "Lord, this situation is too big for me. I give it to You and believe it will bring You praise."

ASK

"If anything is excellent or praiseworthy, think about such things." What can you praise God for right now?

_____

_____

"JUST LIKE YOU" / Music and Lyrics by Angela Donadio
From "It's A New Day"

Winds of change and uncertainty
Do their best to get the best of me
Still in this fragile place here I'm finding
And in this lonely space I'm reminded

(Chorus)
It's just like You to break through
It's just like You to show up
When I least expect it
never guess what You will do
It's just like You to break through
It's just like You to show me that
You're always faithful
It's just like You

When this trial would beg me to
Choose denial I run to You
By Your mercy and grace I'm blind sided
Into Your warm embrace I'm invited

(Bridge)
Give me the eyes of a child
So I can see for miles
Far beyond what my heart can dream
Give me the faith to believe
You're everything that I need
No matter how bad this day may seem

(Chorus)

"It's A New Day" Available on www.angeladonadio.com and iTunes

Session 9

The Best-kept Secret

JOY IN CONTENTMENT
PHILIPPIANS CHAPTER 4

DAY 1 / LIVING AS AN OPEN BOOK—THE VALUE
OF MENTORING—CH 4:9

DAY 2 / LEARNING THE SECRET—CH 4:10-13

DAY 3 / SHARING IN TROUBLES—PAUL'S JOURNEYS
—CH 4:14-16

DAY 4 / MEETING EVERY NEED—CH 4:18-20

DAY 5 / CLOSING REMARKS AND FINAL GREETINGS
—CH 4:21-23

Living as an Open Book—The Value of Mentoring

PHILIPPIANS 4:9

TODAY'S VERSE

> *"Whatever you have learned or received or heard from me, or seen in me*—put it into practice. And the God of peace will be with you."
>
> —Philippians 4:9

Joy-thirsty women, we have come to the last of our study together. I hope you have grown in knowledge, insight and understanding by studying Philippians. In today's verse, Paul reaffirms that his life is an open book, on display for all to see. He is not afraid or ashamed to serve as an example for others to follow. I pray, dear sisters, that we can say the same.

AMPLIFY

JEHOVAH SHALOM—THE LORD IS PEACE

Today's verse encourages us to model our lives after godly men and women like Paul. We'll explore the value of mentoring in a moment. But first, what does Paul share as our reward for "putting this into practice"?

_____

_____

Paul assures us that we will experience the same result in our lives as he has in his. Beautiful girls, we can receive no greater promise than to know we have the peace of God. **When we crave God's heart, peace settles into every crevice of ours.**

In Philippians Chapter 4:4-7, we studied the role peace plays in our life. What did we learn?

_____

_____

In Judges Chapters 6 and 7 we meet Gideon, an interesting character who has a lot to teach us about peace. God orchestrated a divine encounter to confirm His calling to this unlikely hero—plagued by doubt and fear. Not only did God assure him he would be a mighty deliverer of his people, He provided a series of signs to comfort Gideon's feeble heart. As God proved that He was truly calling Gideon to a monumental assignment, Gideon responded by ascribing a name to God: "Jehovah Shalom."

What does Judges 6:24 tell us this name of God means?

_____

_____

The names of God tell us who God is and what He does. Shalom, from the Hebrew, "Shalem," means to be *"complete or sound."* "Shalom" means *peace or absence of strife.* It is the foundation of our modern concept of having peace of mind, or being of sound mind. Women, God wants us to be in peace, not in pieces! Take a moment to read the thrilling conclusion to Gideon's story in Judges Chapter 7. God required Gideon to be completely dependent on Him to bring the victory against the opposition. The massive armies of the Midianites and Amalekites were as thick as locusts, boasting uncountable camels. Gideon started with an army of 32,000 men. When God reduced it, how many remained?

_____

_____

Put yourself in his position for a minute. Gideon was up against insurmountable odds; however, he was victorious with a ludicrous assortment of 300 men, trumpets, and jars. Gideon settled in his heart that he served Jehovah Shalom, giving him valor and peace to face this intimidating task. God has a divine assignment with your name on it; and He will give you the courage and peace you need to complete it.

MODELING

Paul places a premium on mentoring, intentionally leaving a legacy for others to follow. He is comfortable with his life on exhibition, including his beliefs and his practical Christian living. He invites his readers in Philippi to take everything they have learned about him, received from him, and seen in him and put it into practice.

It's important for us to examine what we model for others. Our formal beliefs indicate what we say we believe to be true, but our functional beliefs demonstrate what we practice. When the two are incongruent, we say we believe one thing, but we do another. This can especially prove to be true in parenting. If a parent is not cautious, many things can contribute to defaulting to a "do what I say, not what I do" approach. Inconsistency brings confusion to others and mars the name of Christ. God doesn't ask us for perfection, but an authentic commitment to truth.

Look at today's verse, Philippians 4:9.

In what four ways does Paul allow his life to serve as an example?

1. _____
2. _____
3. _____
4. _____

Let's explore these four ways modeling takes place:

1. Learn—Implies something *taught* to you; you have learned through study or observation of behavior.

   What does this require of the person modeling?

   _____
   _____

What does this require of the person learning?

_____

_____

2. Received—Implies something *given* to you, through intentional investment.
   What does this require of the person modeling?

   _____

   _____

   What does this require of the person receiving?

   _____

   _____

3. Heard—Implies something *spoken* and taught verbally. This can include words spoken directly to you, or words you have heard. Keep in mind that how you say something can be just as important as what you say.

   What does this require of the person modeling?

   _____

   _____

   What does this require of the person hearing?

   _____

   _____

4. Seen—Implies something *displayed* in a way watched and observed by others. This consists of visibly demonstrating Christian character through actions.

   What does this require of the person modeling?

   _____

   _____

   What does this require of the person observing?

   _____

   _____

APPLY

THE VALUE OF MENTORING

We need mature women to teach and mentor our younger women. We also need older men to instill godly principles and share life experiences with younger men. The younger generation must position themselves in a place of learning, just as Timothy did with Paul. To be a Paul, you must deliberately model a life of faith and obedience for others. To be a Timothy, you must be teachable and eager to serve. Allow wise, godly people to speak into your life, giving counsel and direction. It is essential that we have women in our lives to help hold us accountable in our walk with Christ. And girls, as we are ministering to other women and sharing our lives with them, let's remember to keep things in confidence.

ASK

Are you comfortable with your life on display? Consider each of the following areas as invitations for others to model their life after yours. Use the answers you gave to the questions above as your criteria for honest reflection. Pay close attention to any areas you need the Lord's direction and insight.

What others learn from you:

_____

_____

What others receive from you:

_____

_____

What others hear from you:

_____

_____

What others see in you:

_____

_____

Prayer Challenge: *Thank You, Jesus, for the example You have given me to follow. I want my life to glorify You in every way. I pray that what others see in me honors You. Help me to lay my fear at the foot of Your cross, and trust You to be my Jehovah Shalom, My God of Peace.*

Learning the Secret

PHILIPPIANS CHAPTER 4:10-12

TODAY'S VERSE

"I rejoice greatly in the Lord that at last you have renewed your concern for me. Indeed, you have been concerned, but you had no opportunity to show it. I am not saying this because I am in need, for I have learned to be content whatever the circumstances. I know what it is to be in need, and I know what it is to have plenty. I have learned the secret of being content in any and every situation, whether well fed or hungry, whether living in plenty or in want."
— Philippians 4:10-12

A GRATEFUL HEART

Paul dedicated his life to the message of the Gospel, regardless of the personal, professional, or financial cost. In today's verse, why does Paul express that he "rejoices greatly in the Lord"?

_____

_____

Paul's primary purpose in writing the book of Philippians was to express his gratitude for the financial support they sent upon hearing of his detention in Rome. Although he is truly appreciative of it, he is not dependent upon their resources for the work of the ministry to be completed. Earlier, we studied Philippians Chapter 2:19-30. What fellow worker did we meet in this passage that delivered ministry resources from the church in Philippi to Paul while he was in Rome?

_____

_____

Paul continues this thought, discussing his ministry resources in detail in the remaining verses of Philippians Chapter 4. Before he does however, he pauses to let his readers in on a secret.

I HAVE LEARNED THE SECRET

What secret has Paul learned?

- How to be a great preacher
- How to win friends and influence people
- How to be content
- How to be bitten by a snake, shipwrecked, thrown in prison and live to tell about it.

Why do you believe we can struggle with contentment?

_____

_____

"Contentment" means *showing satisfaction with things as they are.* In verse 12, Paul makes the bold declaration, "I have learned the secret of being content in any and every situation." Paul's key to joy is not contingent upon external circumstances. He refuses to allow them to dictate his internal compass. If you'll point your compass north toward contentment, you'll find joy even through the thickest fog.

CONTEXT AND CONTRASTS

Under house arrest and separated from his churches, Paul writes with integrity that he is not in need. Women, I will be honest; Paul's outlook on his circumstances challenges me to my core. Too often, I transfer wants into the needs column. I have said on numerous occasions, "I really need a pedicure" or "I need a vacation." Although welcome treats, they hardly constitute a need.

In what ways does Paul statement challenge you today?

_____

_____

The Bible is full of contrasts. The Old and New Testaments contrast good and evil, wise and foolish choices, and divine or destroyed destinies. Paul uses stark contrasts to describe what he means by "being content in every circumstance."

List the three contrasts here:

_____

_____

Each of these has to do with physical provision. If you have ever found yourself in a comparable situation to Paul, describe that experience.

_____

_____

How can times of scarcity in physical provision cause us to become more dependent on God as our ultimate source?

_____

_____

Contentment is part of the divine equation for finding joy. Avoid the trap of dissatisfaction by pursuing righteousness. We learn the secret of being content by keeping our eyes on eternity.

APPLY

Okay, girls, let's talk about being discontent. It literally means *longing for something better than the present situation; showing or experiencing dissatisfaction or restless longing.* Discontent is a very close relative to "disappointment" which is *a feeling of dissatisfaction that results when your expectations are not realized.* Things in life rarely unfold like we thought they would. **The root of every conflict is unmet expectations.** We project expectations onto people or situations based on our internal needs. Sometimes, expectations become unhealthy, resulting in us becoming too dependent on externals for our source of joy.

Expectations find their foundation in what we believe we are entitled to. A disconnect can exist between what we expect to happen and reality. When this happens, disappointment and discontent can settle in. Some people live their entire lives in a state of discontent.

Based on what have read in our study today, what "state" are you living in?

_____

_____

Joy-thirsty women, if discontent is an area of weakness for you, focus on an attitude of gratitude. Thank God with your thoughts and words throughout your day. Invite Him to reveal Himself and to bring His purposes out of every situation. This will give you a new perspective on life, reframing the curveballs it often throws. Don't be surprised if God moves you into some uncomfortable places. He does this to stretch you, causing you to be completely dependent on Him as your source.

ASK

How is God currently stretching you?

_____

_____

The Secret Revealed

PHILIPPIANS CHAPTER 4:10-13

TODAY'S VERSE

"I rejoice greatly in the Lord that at last you have renewed your concern for me. Indeed, you have been concerned, but you had no opportunity to show it. I am not saying this because I am in need, for I have learned to be content whatever the circumstances. I know what it is to be in need, and I know what it is to have plenty. I have learned the secret of being content in any and every situation, whether well fed or hungry, whether living in plenty or in want. I can do everything through him who gives me strength."

—Philippians 4:10-13

_____

As we studied Chapter 4:10-12, we discovered that Paul learned the secret of being content. This isn't a secret you'll want to keep to yourself; instead, share it with other joy-thirsty women!

AMPLIFY

We find the secret to Paul's joy in Chapter 4:13. Write the verse below in the space provided.

_____

_____

This is perhaps one of the most quoted verses in all of Scripture. My daughter has it inscribed on her bedroom wall. You may even have it memorized. Here it is in a couple different translations:

"I can do all things through Christ which strengtheneth me" — King James Version

"I have strength for all things in Christ Who empowers me [I am ready for anything and equal to anything through Him Who [a] infuses inner strength into me; I am self-sufficient in Christ's sufficiency]" —The Amplified Bible

Why does this verse encourage us as believers?

_____

_____

Paul finds all he needs in and through Christ Jesus. Jesus Christ gives him the strength to overcome an onslaught of adversity. Women, we are overcomers in Christ Jesus. No matter what we go through – confusion, failure, sickness—God never leaves us. Learning the secret of being content is a process requiring commitment and unwavering faith in a loving God. Disappointment and discontentment are two of the biggest rivals you will face in your pursuit of finding—and staying in—joy. I a moment, we'll look at five principles for learning the secret of contentment. But before we do, turn to Numbers Chapter 11, and read the story I have entitled, "The Graves of Craving."

God used Moses to deliver His people out of slavery in Egypt. Now in their second year of the wilderness, God miraculously provided food for the Israelites daily through manna from heaven. In Numbers Chapter 11, we learn about "the rabble," a mixture of diverse cultures that share one common characteristic: they are discontent. The desert air is thick with the familiar sound of their complaints, angering the Lord and resulting in fire breaking out in the camp. Moses prays in response, and the fire dies down. Give your best eye-witness account:

What takes place in verse 4?

_____

_____

What does it say they remember about Egypt?

_____

_____

What does verse 10 tell us Moses heard?

_____

_____

What is it they want?

_____

_____

What is God's response, given in verses 18-20?

_____

_____

Why does God respond this way? (Verse 20 holds the key)

_____

_____

What does verse 31 tell us about the amount of quail God gave?

_____

_____

What is the tragic consequence of their complaining against God, which occurs in Verse 33?

_____

_____

What did they name the place?

_____

_____

Why?

_____

_____

What a catastrophic ending to this chapter in Israel's history. Instead of celebrating God's provision through manna, the rebellious Israelites disintegrate into discontent. Their vehement complaints lead them down a path that winds through Egypt. In Verse 5 they cry, *"We remember the fish we ate in Egypt at no cost—also the cucumbers, melons, leeks, onions, and garlic."*

This verse contains three small words that stop me in my tracks. What do you think they are?

_____

_____

Over two million Israelites spent 400 years enslaved under cruel bondage in Egypt. Now, with rumbling stomachs and discontent spirits over their steady diet of manna, they begin to crave the rich food of Egypt, forgetting the hefty price tag. "At no cost," they erroneously reminiscence. Slavery always has a cost. Sin always has a cost. And the cost of their discontent? The Promised Land. The Israelites spent forty years in the wilderness due to their disobedience. But the barrier to the Promised Land wasn't the wilderness; it was their wandering. They wandered through discontent and disbelief to the burial site, "Kibroth Hattaavah," which means "the graves of craving." Tragically, it was here the Israelites dug graves for their fellow brothers and sisters who had craved other food.

Dear sisters, how desperately I want you to avoid the grave of craving in your own life. Just like Eve in the Garden, we are tempted to crave what we don't have: a different body, house, job, spouse...even a different life. The issue is internal, not external. Changing your surroundings will never bring you joy if you're not grounded in the person of Jesus Christ. The secret to finding joy is finding our identity in Christ alone.

APPLY

These principles will help you avoid the grave of craving by learning contentment in all circumstances.

1. Contentment comes when we yield completely to God.
2. Contentment comes when we trust the timing of God.
3. Contentment comes when we rest in the faithfulness of God.
4. Contentment comes when we depend on the grace of God.

5. Contentment comes when we focus on the promise of eternity with God.

ASK

Take a moment and identify any areas where disappointment and discontentment threaten to strangle your joy. Painful events can lead us to blame God. Even though God cannot disappoint, you may feel disappointed by God. You can share your deepest emotions with Him. He can handle it. In fact, He invites you to do that very thing: press your pain into the heart of Jesus. You're safe in His capable hands. **Remember, our disappointments are God's appointments.**

_____

_____

_____

_____

Prayer Challenge: *I can do all things through You. Thank You for Your strength working in me as I stay yielded to You. Thank You for teaching me the secret of being content and resting in You. The joy of the Lord is my strength.*

Sharing in Troubles and Meeting Every Need

PHILIPPIANS CHAPTER 4:14-20

TODAY'S VERSE

"Yet it was good of you to share in my troubles. Moreover, as you Philippians know, in the early days of your acquaintance with the Gospel, when I set out from Macedonia, not one church shared with me in the matter of giving and receiving, except you only; for even when I was in Thessalonica, you sent me aid again and again when I was in need. Not that I am looking for a gift, but I am looking for what may be credited to your account. I have received full payment and even more; I am amply supplied, now that I have received from Epaphroditus the gifts you sent. They are a fragrant offering, an acceptable sacrifice, pleasing to God. And my God will meet all your needs according to his glorious riches in Christ Jesus. To our God and Father be glory for ever and ever. Amen". —Philippians 4:14-20

As we near the end of our study together, how fitting that today's lesson is a bit of Paul's walk down memory lane. In this passage, he highlights significant seasons of his ministry when the church of Philippi was a fountain of tremendous blessing to him. We will look at these key periods in his life, noting what he experienced because of his partnership with the Philippian church.

AMPLIFY

SHARING IN TROUBLES

The words of Chapter 4:14-20 are laced with loneliness. All of us, at one time or another, may wrestle with feelings of isolation. Unfortunately, Paul is intimately acquainted with these unwelcome companions of ministry. Remember, girlfriends, this is long before the age of the internet and text messages that travel the globe. Paul underwent months without hearing a familiar voice, ministering for lengthy periods without a companion. We have seen throughout our study of Philippians the high premium Paul placed on the value of partnership in ministry.

What phrases in today's verses reflect a tone of loneliness, conveying the sentiment that Paul is out on a limb alone?

_____

_____

Who is the only church that gave him financial support when he set out from Macedonia?

_____

_____

What effect do you believe this had on Paul's feelings toward the church in Philippi?

_____

_____

What is the name of the person mentioned in today's verse that brought the ministry gifts to Paul from Philippi? (We have studied him before)

_____

_____

What does Philippians 2:19-30 tell us about what happened to him in his quest to bring funds and supplies to Paul?

_____

_____

Imagine being in Paul's shoes; far from the comforts of home, away from family and friends, and hampered by limited financial resources. His plight only continued to sour by being chained to a Roman guard twenty-four hour a day. Under these circumstances, what might it mean to Paul to have a friend visit him, bringing news from home, fresh supplies, and a financial blessing?

_____

_____

MACEDONIA AND THESSALONICA

In the passage we are studying, Paul references the early days of his acquaintance with the church members in Philippi. You can read about this season of his life in Acts 16 and 17. Macedonia was the northern part of modern day Greece where Berea, Thessalonica, and Philippi were located. Philippi was a Roman colony and the leading city of the District of Macedonia. In these chapters, he sets out from Macedonia for the South (Achaia), where Athens and Corinth were located.

What key event happened while Paul was ministering with Silas in Acts 16?

_____

_____

What stands out the most to you in this story about Paul's ministry and why?

_____

_____

Acts 17 records Paul's short visit to Thessalonica. Paul also thanks the church in Philippi for repeatedly supporting him while he was there during his second missionary journey. Due to the rise of violent persecution, Paul left the city quickly to ensure his own safety and the protection of his converts. Paul sent Timothy from Athens back to Thessalonica to encourage the church and report to Paul on their progress. The books of 1st and 2nd Thessalonians are letters Paul wrote to them based on Timothy's reports. While under tremendous persecution in Thessalonica, he received ongoing support from his converts in Philippi. It encouraged him to know that his ministry, although under heavy opposition, was not in vain. The church in Philippi stood out to Paul for many reasons, including their love, prayer, and financial support. They served as a beacon of light, shining into some of Paul's darkest moments.

Perhaps, like Paul, someone's prayer or financial support has blessed you. They may have "shared in your troubles" and helped to meet a need. If this is the case, whom did God use in your life, and how did that shape who you are today?

_____

_____

CREDITED TO YOUR ACCOUNT

In Chapter 4:18, Paul makes a very interesting statement about the funds they bring him. Rather than looking for a gift, he tells his readers that he is "looking for what may be credited to your account." These words provide us another glimpse into Paul's others-minded worldview. Amid difficulty, including financial strain, Paul's overarching concern is always for others.

He describes their "gift" in three ways. What are they?

_____

_____

What blessing does Paul promise the church of Philippi because of their partnership with him?

_____

_____

APPLY

The apostle Paul's life is an exquisite tapestry of carefully chosen threads, woven together by a loving God. This tapestry includes every person Paul met, every place Paul visited, and every experience Paul shared. God placed people in Paul's path to both bless and receive from him. We reap the benefits of learning from their example and following in their footsteps.

From our study together, who are a few of these people?

_____

_____

Who did you enjoy getting to know the most and why?

_____

_____

Women, God connects us to each other because He created us for relationship. **We are here to complete one another; not compete with one another.** We find joy even when life is out of focus by watching for ways we can "share in someone else's troubles." Look through an others-oriented lens, searching for opportunities to link arms with another joy-thirsty woman. God's grace will saturate your sacrifice and you'll love the life you see.

God is embroidering a personalized masterpiece with your name on it, incomplete without the colorful threads of soul-enriching relationships. The beauty of it all is that as you pour into someone else, God responds by blessing you—meeting your every need according to His riches in Christ Jesus. He adorns you with wisdom and crowns you with strength. That, my sweet friend, is a woman filled with joy.

ASK

Reflect on the carefully chosen threads in your own life. How has God used people and situations to draw you closer to Him? Consider following in the footsteps of Paul, writing a letter to thank them for the ways they've impacted your life.

_____

_____

_____

_____

Closing Remarks and Final Greetings

PHILIPPIANS CHAPTER 4:21-23

TODAY'S VERSE

> *"Greet all the saints in Christ Jesus. The brothers who are with me send greetings. All the saints send you greetings, especially those who belong to Caesar's household. The grace of the Lord Jesus Christ be with your spirit. Amen".* —Philippians 4:21-23

Dear sisters in Christ, I can hardly believe we have come to the last day of our journey together. We have discovered new reservoirs of joy by studying Philippians. I pray God has spoken to you through the pages of His Word and through this study. Believe me when I say that I have prayed for you every step of the way, often using Philippians 1:9-11: "And this is my prayer: that your love may abound more and more in knowledge and depth of insight so that you may be able to discern what is best and may be blameless until the day of Christ, filled with the fruit of righteousness that comes through Jesus Christ to the glory of God."

Joy-thirsty women, God will honor the commitment you've shown by applying His Word to your heart. He will accomplish His purpose in your life as you continue to look through the lens of His perspective. Early on, we studied Paul's opening remarks and first impressions. Today, we conclude by considering his choice of closing remarks and final greetings. Remember, every word in Scripture is inspired and included on purpose.

AMPLIFY

ALL THE SAINTS

Paul sends greetings from the brothers who are with him. These are fellow Jews who have converted through the message of the Gospel. In addition, Paul includes a particular group of people who send their greetings.

Who are they?

_____

_____

THE WHOLE PALACE GUARD

Philippians 1:13 tells us that the "whole palace guard" knows that Paul is in chains for Christ. This includes several thousand Roman soldiers, many of whom have had personal contact with Paul. Not even chains could stop Paul from sharing the Gospel.

What group does Paul give special significance to in today's verse?

_____

_____

Women, those in Caesar's household include members of the guard and others who had a backstage pass at the palace. They have come to Christ through Paul's life and ministry. They have received the gift of salvation as a direct result of Paul's pain.

What are some reasons this would this be of such importance to Paul and to his readers?

_____

_____

One Biblical commentary tells us this about those Paul led to the Lord in Caesar's household: "These are the slaves and dependents of Nero who had been probably converted through Paul's teaching while he was a prisoner in the Prætorian barrack attached to the palace. Philippi was a Roman "colony," hence there might arise a tie between the citizens of the mother city and those of the colony; especially between those of both cities who were Christians, converted as many of them were by the same apostle, and under like circumstances, he having been imprisoned at Philippi, as he now is at Rome."[19]

What does Paul say about the Gospel in 2 Timothy 2:8-10?

_____

_____

By now, you have come to know a great deal about Paul. How does this passage of Scripture enhance your opinion of his character and devotion to the cause of Christ?

APPLY

I've loved giving you a backstage pass into seasons of my life where my joy went into hiding. Together we've studied principles that keep us in joy when life is out of focus. Just as Paul's life impacted those around him, your story needs to be told. Don't be stingy with backstage passes. Share the transforming message of the Gospel with those in your sphere of influence. **God will use your private pain for kingdom gain if you'll allow Him to use your story for His glory.**

Paul seized every opportunity to see others come to the saving knowledge of Jesus Christ. The all-consuming love of Jesus radically saved him and miraculously transformed him. The extravagant gift of grace motivated Paul to reach the lost with the message of the Gospel, no matter what the cost. Joy-thirsty women, this is our Gospel. No set of circumstances can chain it. No amount of adversity can destroy it. I love you for taking this journey with me. I pray you found joy, and I speak over you the final words of this wonderful book: ***"The grace of the Lord Jesus Christ be with you."*** Joy-thirsty women, keep looking through the grace-crafted lens of God's perspective. You'll love the life you see.

"SOLITUDE OF SILENCE" / Music by Angela Donadio and Lyrics by
Dr. Steve Phifer
From "It's A New Day"

In the silence of my soul, Lord, I will seek You
In the stillness of my spirit I must stay
I will flee from all the rush and noise around me
In the solitude of silence, I will wait.

(Chorus)
For Your voice cannot be heard above the clamor
And Your presence does not rest upon our haste
In the silence of my soul I will seek You
In the solitude of silence I will wait.

I will ask the singing winds to serenade me
I will let the sunlight dance upon my fears
Thinking back to all who listened here before me
Silent laughter, silent prayers and silent tears.

(Chorus)

In the pages of the Book Your heart is calling
As the ancient words fall soft upon my ear
Like an early season snowfall cool and healing
Heaven's peace, a glistening blanket, quells my fear.

(Chorus)

"It's A New Day" Available on www.angeladonadio.com and iTunes

YOUR DAMASCUS ROAD STORY...

Finding Joy Leadership Guide

This guide will help you plan and lead this Bible Study. Provide each participant with a book, and encourage them to do the homework daily. The Study is divided into 9 sessions of study. Feel free to shorten or expand the time frame you use to go through the material as needed. (If you need to shorten the study, keep in mind that women will need to do more than one week's worth of homework per week.) Each study includes five daily lessons, each requiring about 20–30 minutes to read and apply through questions and personal prayer challenges. This Study uses the NIV 1983 Bible.

In your small groups, encourage the women to share and discuss what God has been teaching them throughout the study. Small groups are an important way to build relationships, share life experiences, and ensure understanding of the Scriptures being studied. Take time to pray for one another, particularly when the Holy Spirit is using the Study to bring awareness, conviction, and healing. Allow the session to serve as a catalyst for change and action. Information only becomes transformation with application.

This guide offers discussion starters by emphasizing key principles. Pray for the women taking this Study under your leadership, adapting the Guide to best fit their needs, and your style as a discussion facilitator. Ask the Holy Spirit for wisdom, insight, and discernment as you come alongside each participant in their journey through Philippians. For best results, contact the women in your class via phone call or email throughout to encourage and motivate them in their personal growth.

This Study contains lyrics from songs both of my CD Projects—"This Journey" and "It's A New Day". These CD projects will be made available at a discount to Group Leaders by request and are available for purchase at www.angeladonadio.com and on iTunes. Feel free to play the song featured at the end of each week's study at the beginning or ending of your class.

PREPARING TO LEAD

1. Enlist the support of your Pastor and provide details for the church calendar.
2. Promote the Study four to six weeks prior in your church or small group, encouraging women to sign up and purchase books in advance.
3. Offer child care if necessary and if possible.

OPENING SESSION!

1. Have labels for name tags and sharpies for women at the first class. Consider printing "Finding Joy" on each name tag if possible. Welcome women and ask them to fill out their name tags. Have worship music playing softly on a CD or iPod Station in the background to help create a warm atmosphere.
2. Distribute books, pens or pencils at the first class, and have a sign-up sheet or individual sheets for women to fill out with name and contact information.
3. Offer coffee, tea, water, and light refreshments. Participants can rotate bringing a snack for class.
4. Introduce yourself and any assistants, and ask the women to introduce themselves with one sentence about who they are. (This sets up one of the homework sessions in the first week). The opening session will set the tone for your Study, so consider doing an eight to ten minute "ice breaker" with the women. The internet offers a large variety of activities which inspire women to get to know one another in a fun, non-threatening way. Another fun activity is to take the words "Finding Joy When Life is Out of Focus" and give them five minutes to see how many words they can create from the title. Offer a small door prize to the one who comes up with the most words. You get the idea : Just make this first session fun, relaxed, and inviting!
5. Using a marker board, chalk board or poster board (whatever you might have available), ask the women to provide as many details as they can remember about Paul.
6. Let the women know that this study will focus on Paul's life and

his letter to the church at Philippi, Philippians. Ask the women to volunteer answers to the following questions:

- How would you define joy?
- What would you say are "sources" of joy?
- What steals your joy?

7. If time remains, feel free to begin with the Introduction, explaining the "3 A's" Study Method. Pray and conclude class.

SESSION 1

Playlist: "Trust You Anyhow" from "This Journey" if you would like to open or close class.

1. Provide name tags for any women joining after the first week. Offer refreshments, soft music and a short ice breaker if you so desire.
2. If time did not allow you to explain the 3 A's at the first class, discuss the Study Method at this point. Ask if there are any questions or comments concerning the Study Method. (Introduction)
3. Ask the women what "frame", if any, Angela's testimony provided for their journey into Philippians. Inquire if any of the women identified with Angela's struggles with physical adversity. If so, ask if any would like to share briefly with the class (try to keep this to just a couple of minutes to avoid women monopolizing conversation and discussion). Ask for their responses to this question found in Day 2: How can God use the U-turns, detours, and dead ends in your life to bring glory to Him?
4. Draw their attention to Day 3, "Paul's Opening Remarks and First Impressions". Remind them that they introduced themselves the previous week. Considering the study, how might they introduce themselves differently?
5. From Day 4, discuss the principles found in the section titled "Created for Relationship". What changes were any women prompted to make in their relationships due to these insights?
6. Ask if there were any questions about this week's study. If so, take time to look at those areas. Pray and conclude class. Seeing Paul's instruction and importance on prayer, consider how you can give this special focus.

SESSION 2

Playlist: "Joy" from "It's A New Day" if you would like to open or close class.

1. Consider offering fruit for refreshments, or a display of fruit for discussion. Ask the women to share about their favorite kind of fruit.
2. Ask if there were any questions about this week's study. If so, take time to look at those areas. Why is surrender such a struggle for us? What are some of the benefits when we surrender?
3. From Day 1, discuss the concept of fruit in our lives. Picturing their life as a tree, what type of fruit is adorning the branches? What fruit is missing?
4. From Day 2, ask the women to describe practical ways their life would be impacted by being chained to a guard 24 hours a day. Ask them to give their answers to the question "What might you be tempted to think, feel or say if you were in Paul's shoes?".
5. From "Clothing Yourself With Courage", ask what they chose to place under God's Character. Discuss.

   Pray and conclude class.

SESSION 3

Playlist: "It's A New Day" from "It's A New Day" if you would like to open or close class.

1. Come prepared to bring or describe one of your most prized possessions. *Consider bringing a photo of a loved one rather than an item of great monetary value.
2. From Day 1, "Most Prized Possession"—Ask if anyone has ever lost a valuable possession? Describe. What was Paul's most prized possession?
3. From Day 2, "Your Choices Matter," ask women to volunteer which category they identified with most and why. Volunteer to read what you wrote for the following questions:
   • What would your obituary say about you if it was written right now?"
   • What do you want it to say?
   • Ask if anyone would like to volunteer their answers to these questions, and how this impacted them.
4. From Day 3, "Overdrawn or Overflowing?", what items did you identify as making "withdrawals" of your Joy Account? What items make "deposits"? *Consider writing "JOY ACCOUNT" on a marker board,

chalkboard or poster board, and list some of their answers in each column.

5. From Day 4, "On Your Best Behavior," discuss the armor listed in Ephesians 6. Ask the women to share which piece of armor stood out to them and why.

6. From Day 5, "Granted Suffering," ask for their thoughts and reactions. What are our responses to the "uninvited guest" of suffering? Considering today's passage, how might you view "endured suffering" as a compliment? Emphasize that Paul is referring to suffering as being a direct result of his stand for Christ. *This can be a challenging topic to navigate. Try to keep the conversation centered on this passage, and how it relates to us in our Christian walk. Avoid allowing discussion to become divisive.

SESSION 4

Playlist: "A Woman in Love" from "This Journey" if you would like to open or close class.

1. Why do you think unity is so important to God?

2. From Day 2, "The VIP Treatment," discuss the "wardrobe" provided for us in Colossians 3:12-14. Consider having a little fun with this week's theme. You could bring items of clothing as "wardrobe", label them with the characteristics, and "dress" someone in class. These can be simple items such as a hat, scarf, jacket, etc... You could also just display wardrobe items, or bring dressier items a "VIP" might wear. The idea is to provide a "VIP" atmosphere. Yards of inexpensive red fabric felt can serve as a "red carpet" as women arrive, and greeting women to walk down the carpet as a "VIP". Have fun! Women will remember the point!

3. From Day 3, "A Picture of Humility," ask women to discuss which area was the most challenging for them this week: A renewed mind, a guarded tongue, or a submitted spirit.

4. From Day 4, "Jesus as Servant," and Day 5, "A New Song, "ask for responses in Application of John 13. Depending on the format, size and nature of your class, prayerfully consider having a time to wash their feet. This can be a very powerful, personal experience, if you are comfortable leading your women in this experience. You may also consider setting aside a time after class, or another time where you invite women who would like to a foot-washing ceremony. You will

need individual basins, water and towels. Please feel no pressure to do this, but I want to give you options and ideas to pray over.

Another powerful experience for women, perhaps as an alternative, is to have a piece of wood and a hammer, representing Christ's obedience to the cross. Have women take small slips of paper and write an area of their life they want to surrender to the Lord (it can even be from the above question—a renewed mind, a guarded tongue, or a submitted spirit). While playing soft worship music in the background, invite women to "nail" their papers to the wood, giving them to the Lord and putting them under the blood of Jesus.

As you can see, this week's class can go a variety of directions. You may want to incorporate one of these ideas into a different class, or hold a foot-washing at a separate time or the Celebration week. You could also make the Celebration week the "VIP" Treatment. These are simply suggestions to guide you in creating an atmosphere where God can reveal Himself to the beautiful women taking your class. Commit to prayer how God would have you lead the women He has entrusted to you for this Study. The Holy Spirit will give you wisdom, insight and discernment.

Pray and conclude class.

SESSION 5

Playlist: "Poured Out" from "It's a New Day" if you would like to open or close class.

1. From Day 1, "Obeying on Purpose," what "ingredients" in the recipe found in 2 Peter 1:5-8 did the women find most challenging, or indicate they are missing in their life?
2. From Day 2, "Shine Like Stars," talk about us reflecting the glory of God. Consider bringing a mirror with the phrase "God's Word" taped to it or a glow in the dark toy for discussion starters. Discuss why it is so difficult to "do all things without grumbling and complaining", and practical ways they can shift the atmosphere to praise.
3. From Day 3, "Shine Like Stars Part 2," ask women to offer the purposes they gave for the light sources listed. Consider bringing a couple of unusual light sources; a lantern, flashlight or decorative lamp for discussion of the purposes of light. Perhaps change the lighting look in the room during discussion.
4. From Day 4, "Poured Out," ask if the women had any questions

concerning the OT Offerings. From Day 5, "A Support System," talk about the importance of living in community in our Christian walk. Discuss the need for a support system, encouraging the women to seek out others to mentor them or to mentor, depending on where they are in their walk with Christ. Ask them to share any new insights they learned by reading more about Timothy and Epaphroditus.

Pray and conclude class.

SESSION 6

Playlist: "Invisible" from "This Journey" if you would like to open or close class.

1. From Day 1, "Safeguard Your Joy," discuss reactions to Hannah's sacrifice and willingness to obey regardless of her personal loss. How has God transformed a situation in someone's life? Invite someone to share their response.
2. From Day 2, "A New Heart," discuss the four promises God gives us in Ezekiel 36:26. Discuss the items they added to the lists of a heart of stone and a heart of flesh. Point out the differences between a stone (dead) and a real human heart (alive). Ask them to compare aloud and discuss the spiritual analogy in-depth.
3. From Day 3, "Paul's Resume on File," be prepared to share your Damascus Road experience you wrote. Ask if anyone would like to share theirs in class. You may want to ask them in advance, or consider asking women to share in pairs or small groups of three or four. Use your discretion as to what would work best with the dynamics of your class.
4. From Day 4, "The Great Reversal," discuss what Paul was willing to lose for the sake of Christ.
5. From Day 5, "Living Dead," discuss the four areas of "knowing Christ" Paul identifies in today's verses. What does "Living Dead" mean to you?

The focal point of this week is finding our identity in Christ rather than external things. Ask the Holy Spirit to guide you in any activities that support or reinforce this truth.

SESSION 7

Playlist: "Nail Pierced Hands" from "It's A New Day" if you would like to open or close class.

1. From Day 1, Pressing Toward the Prize," discuss "forgetting what is behind." Ask for their responses on the pitfalls of getting stuck in the past, either positive or negative memories. How can we get victory over our past?
2. From Day 2, "Following the Pattern," consider bringing a pattern into class. Ask women to share the patterns they drew of the characteristics in their own lives.
3. From Day 3, "Distraught over a Derailed Destiny," discuss the progression of the verbs walk, stand, and sit, from Psalm 1. Discuss how sin takes us from walking to standing and sitting, exploring the practical application of this truth. What does this tell us about the power of our choices?
4. If you have time, discuss for a couple of minutes about each area Paul lists in a derailed destiny: god is their stomach, glory is in their shame, and their mind is on earthly things. Which area impacted them the most and why? If they took time to write verses from Isaiah 61, have a couple of women share what meant the most to them.
5. From Day 4, "Divine Destiny", discuss "Body," "Mind," and "Soul/ Spirit." What specifics did they add to the lists? Ask if they had any questions about decision making, and if anyone used the questions concerning a pressing decision. If so, in what ways did the questions help them? Consider printing the "HALT" acronym on a 3x5 card to give women.
6. From Day 5, "Eyes Up!", ask what they are most looking forward to about heaven. What meant the most to them about the hymn, "Trust and Obey." Consider singing it aloud as a group.

SESSION 8

Playlist: "Just Like You" from "It's A New Day" if you would like to open or close class.

1. From Day 1, "Stand Firm," discuss the question, "Why does knowing more about our Heavenly Father enable us to place greater trust in Him?"
2. From Day 2, "A Woman of Influence," discuss the women that blessed Paul's ministry. Ask them why they felt these women, Euodia and

Syntyche, were singled out. Do they agree that they were women of influence? What were some of the things listed alongside of "gossip" in Romans 1:28-32?

3. How does Matthew 18 teach us to handle conflict?

4. From Day 3, "The Promise of Peace," which of the 5 instructions impacted or challenged you most and why? Discuss the concept of "boundaries" and why God gives them for our good. Healthy boundaries are necessary for our own health and for the health of our relationships with others. Living within God-designed boundaries (found in His Word) guards us and gives us peace.

5. From Day 4, "Decorating Others," share ideas of how we can decorate others with our words. For fun, consider decorating cupcakes or a cake together, then eating them as your snacks.　Discuss the principle of justice being God's domain. When we demand justice, demanding our own rights, we put ourselves in the place of God. When our internal justice scale is violated, if we don't surrender it to God, we attempt to take justice into our own hands. Ask if the women had any questions about this principle and clarify.

6. From Day 5, "A Good Report", discuss the story in Numbers 13 and 14, using the questions provided in the lesson.

SESSION 9

Playlist: "Solitude of Silence" from "It's A New Day" if you would like to open or close class.

1. From Day 1, "Living as an Open Book—The Value of Mentoring," write the following acronym for "MENTOR" on a white board and/or on 3x5 cards for each participant. Encourage the women to volunteer their insights on what qualities exemplify a godly mentor. Discuss mentoring and the value of modeling an exemplary Christian life.

   Here is an acronym for **MENTOR** to help us see the role of a mentor:
   - **M**—Mother (Spiritual mother)
   - **E**—Experience (Sharing and learning from Life experience)
   - **N**—Nurturer
   - **T**—Tested Teacher
   - **O**—Open-ended questions (vs. closed "yes" or "no" questions; Guide toward self-discovery rather than just giving advice)
   - **R**—Raises and releases others

2. From Day 2, "Learning the Secret," discuss the rivals to joy, discontentment and disappointment. Ask the women to share their thoughts and feelings about unmet expectations and how God is stretching them. For fun, give each woman a rubber band.

3. From Day 3, "The Secret Revealed," discuss the story in Numbers 11, "The Graves of Craving". We tend to look back and crave something God has delivered us from, without remembering the cost of what He has delivered us from. Ask the women why they believe this is the case, and what we can do to avoid this pitfall in our walk as believers. Highlight the five principles I give to avoid the graves of craving, asking the women to share which impacted them the most and why.

4. From Day 4, "Sharing in Troubles and Meeting Every Need," focus on loneliness, the joy of friendship through Epaphroditus and the Philippian church, and their own experiences in being blessed by someone while in need. Who have they enjoyed getting to know the most? Consider handing out assorted colors of threads to the women reminding them of the beautiful tapestry God is weaving of their life.

5. From Day 5, "Closing Remarks and Final Greetings," ask the women to share any closing thoughts about the journey to "Finding Joy." Encourage the women to offer others a Backstage Pass into their life. Celebrate the conclusion of your journey together!

Endnotes

1. Charles Stanley, "Living Above Circumstances," In Touch Ministries, March 7, 2011.
2. New International Version Bible, revised in August 1983, Colorado Springs, CO
3. New International Version Bible, revised in August 1983, Colorado Springs, CO
4. New International Version Bible, revised in August 1983, Colorado Springs, CO
5. Pauline epistles, www.wikipedia.org
6. Reinhard Bonnke, www.azquotes.com
7. Corrie ten Boom, www.crosswalk.com
8. New International Version Bible, revised in August 1983, Colorado Springs, CO
9. A.W. Tozer, The Pursuit of God: The Human Thirst for the Divine
10. www.businessinsider.com, February 26, 2017.
11. Mother Teresa, www.goodreads.com
12. www.blueletterbible.org
13. www.sciencedaily.com, July 6, 2011.
14. www.biblestudytools.com
15. www.baseballhistorian.com/html/sandy_koufax.htm; www.wikipedia.org/wiki/Curveball
16. www.latindictionary.wikidot.com
17. www.bradfordhealth.com
18. www.psychologytoday.com
19. Robert Jamieson, A Commentary on the Old and New Testaments (3 Volume Set)Hardcover—February 1, 1996)

COMING FALL 2019 FROM
ANGELA DONADIO AND BRIDGE-LOGOS

FEARLESS:
ORDINARY WOMEN OF THE BIBLE WHO DARED EXTRAORDINARY THINGS

MORE ABOUT ANGELA

Angela Donadio
Make Your Life Matter No Matter What

Connect with me!

angeladonadio.com

@angeladonadio

@AngelaDonadioVOV

angela@angeladonadio.com

Subscribe to my blog, **"The M&M's of life"** on my website to receive a weekly dose of encouragement!

Angela Donadio
Make Your Life Matter No Matter What

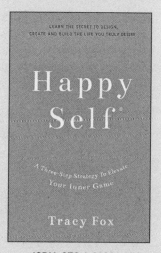

BEAUTY FROM ASHES
Donna Sparks

In a transparent and powerful manner, the author reveals how the Lord took her from the ashes of a life devastated by failed relationships and destructive behavior to bring her into a beautiful and powerful relationship with Him. The author encourages others to allow the Lord to do the same for them.

Donna Sparks is an Assemblies of God evangelist who travels widely to speak at women's conferences and retreats. She lives in Tennessee.

www.story-of-grace.com

www.facebook.com/
  donnasparksministries/

https://www.facebook.com/
  AuthorDonnaSparks/

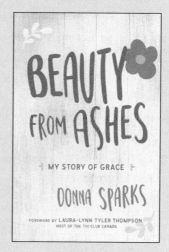

ISBN: 978-1-61036-252-8